**First published in the UK 2023 by Sona Books
an imprint of Danann Media Publishing Ltd.**

© 2023 Danann Media Publishing Limited

WARNING: For private domestic use only, any unauthorised Copying, hiring, lending or public performance of this book is illegal.

Published under licence from Future Publishing Limited a Future PLC group company. All rights reserved. No part of this publication may be reproduced or stored in a retrieval system or transmitted in any form or by any means without the prior written permission of the publisher.

Copy Editor Juliette O'Neill

This is an independent publication and it is unofficial and unauthorised and as such has no connection with Mojang.

© 2022 Future Publishing PLC

CAT NO: SON0549
ISBN: 978-1-915343-09-3

Made in EU.

WELCOME

It's incredible to think that Minecraft has already been around for over ten years and counting – and it just keeps on getting better! There is no other videogame quite like it out there.

It's also a game packed with secrets, intricacies and a huge number of things to do, which is where this handy guide comes in. Over the coming pages, we've crammed in as much as we possibly can about this blocky masterpiece.

We're going to take you right through the basics, then show you how to survive and even thrive in the game. Finally, we finish off with some advanced stuff at the back!

Make sure you're ready for the amazing adventure ahead! And most importantly, make sure you enjoy your time Minecrafting!

Just watch out for creepers…

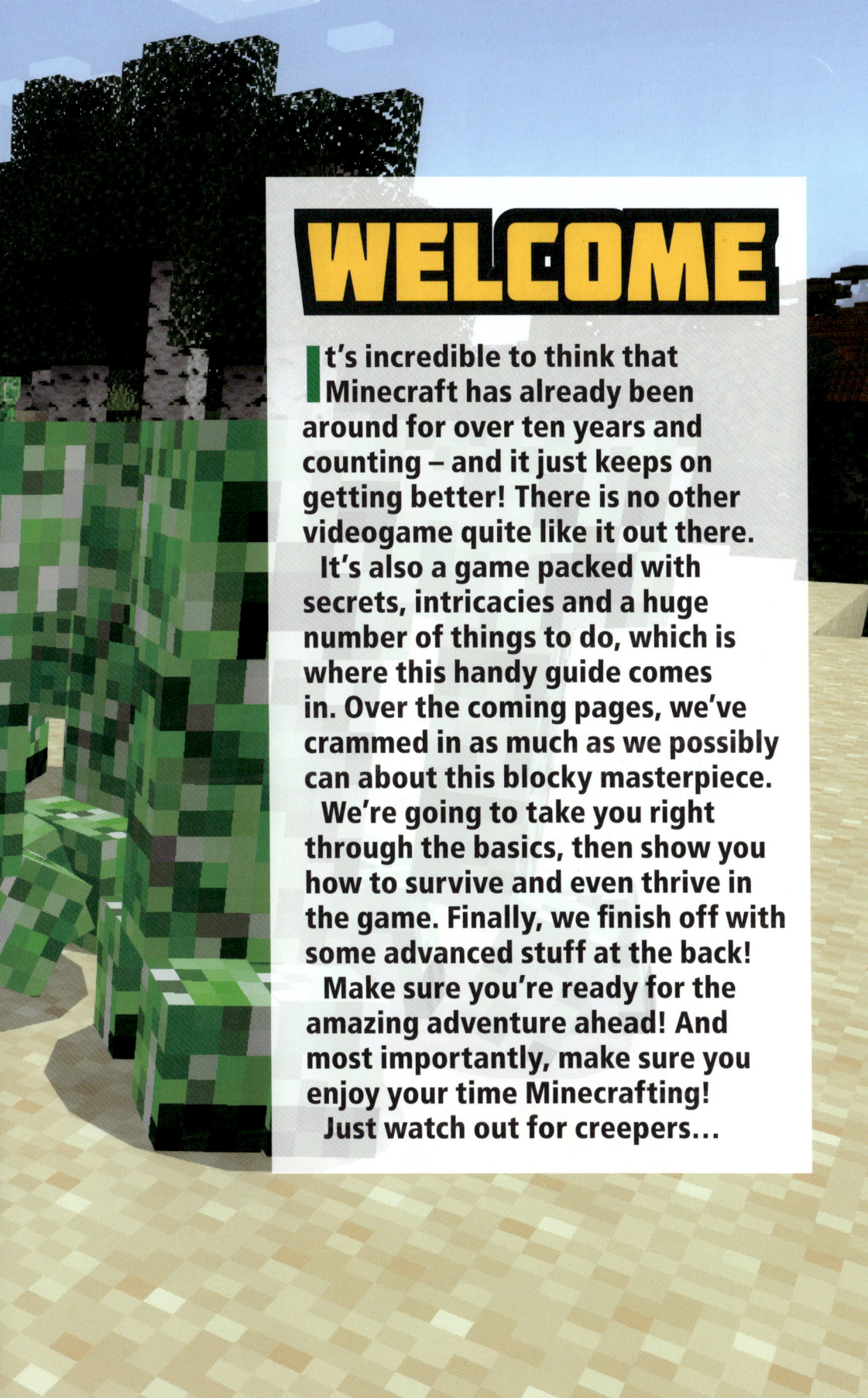

CONTENTS

MINECRAFT BASICS

New to Minecraft? Here are the basics you'll need to know…

10 THE OVERWORLD: A NEED TO KNOW GUIDE

- 12 Blocks
- 13 Items
- 14 Crafting
- 15 Mining
- 16 Sleeping
- 17 Health
- 18 Hunger
- 19 Saturation
- 20 Combat
- 21 Experience
- 22 Friendly Mobs Guide
- 28 Hostile Mobs Guide
- 32 Understanding Mob Drops
- 34 Minecraft Basics Secrets

SURVIVAL TACTICS

Minecraft's Survival mode is tough, so here are some essential tips for staying alive!

- 38 Ore & Resources
- 40 Scavenging Food
- 42 Farming
- 44 Taming Mobs
- 46 Breeding Guide
- 48 Summoning Golems
- 50 Fishing Secrets
- 52 Trading
- 54 Repairing Gear
- 56 Weapon & Armour Secrets
- 58 Job Site Blocks
- 60 Surviving Secrets

38 ORE & RESOURCES

74 MANSIONS

STRUCTURES & EXPLORATION

Minecraft's biomes are filled with structures for you to hunt down and explore, but some are extremely rare!

- 64 Villages
- 65 Igloos
- 66 Witch Huts
- 67 Ruins
- 68 Ocean Monuments
- 69 Shipwrecks
- 70 Jungle Temples
- 71 Desert Temple Secrets
- 72 Finding Fossils
- 73 Dungeons
- 74 Mansions
- 75 Strongholds
- 76 Ruined Portals
- 77 Abandoned Mines
- 78 Pillager Outposts
- 79 Ravines
- 80 Maps & Banners
- 82 Portals
- 84 Biomes
- 86 Structures & Exploration Secrets

THE NETHER & THE END

Now you've mastered the Overworld, it's time to brave the Nether and the End!

90	The Nether: A Need To Know Guide
92	Nether Mobs
94	Nether Biomes
96	Nether Fortresses
98	Bastion Remnants
100	Netherite Gear
102	Reaching The End
104	The End: A Need To Know Guide
106	The Ender Dragon
108	End Cities
109	End Ships
110	Ender Chests
111	Shulker Boxes
112	Elytra

ADVANCED MINECRAFT

Get the most out of your world with our guide to tackling the trickier parts of the game!

128 LIGHT A BEACON

116	Brewing
118	Enchanting Gear
120	Summoning the Wither
122	Pillager Raids
124	Zombie Sieges
126	Conduits
128	Light a Beacon
130	Respawn the Dragon
132	Advanced Secrets

104 THE END: A NEED TO KNOW GUIDE

Night & day

THE OVERWORLD:
A Need to Know Guide

As soon as you enter Minecraft, you land in the Overworld – a rich, near-infinite dimension abundant with life, challenges and secrets to discover in your quest to find and defeat the ender dragon!

YOUR NEW HOME
The Overworld is the most varied and friendly of Minecraft's three dimensions – the Overworld, the Nether and the End. Whether you play alone or with friends, you'll spend most of your time in this dimension exploring its landscape, gathering materials, and creating your own items and structures.

The Overworld is made of blocks and populated by mobs – that's short for "mobiles", meaning anything that has a mind of its own, from fish to creepers to villagers. Some are hostile, some are friendly, and you'll have to learn the difference pretty quickly!

BIOMES
The Overworld is divided into medium-sized "biomes" which have their own properties. A desert biome is mostly made of sand blocks with very few interesting features, while a jungle biome grows thick with plant life. Every biome has its own features, blocks and mobs to look out for – and some are safer than others!

THE OVERWORLD: A NEED TO KNOW GUIDE

NIGHT & DAY
While the Overworld is mostly safe, once the sun sets, hostile mobs can spawn around you. Surviving is much harder at night, which is why it makes sense to build a safe base for yourself with a lit interior where mobs can't spawn. The day-night cycle in Minecraft lasts around 20 minutes, with seven of those being the most dangerous part of the night. Luckily, when the sun comes out, most hostile mobs will either burn up or despawn, rendering the Overworld (mostly) safe again!

LANDSCAPE
One other way the Overworld is different from the real world is that its landscape is near-infinite. Even if you walked in a single direction forever, you'd never reach the edge!

As well as vast seas and lakes, you'll find huge mountains and hills in the Overworld, plus deep ravines and caves that can wind all the way from the surface to bedrock level. The Overworld is 256 blocks high, with sea level at around 65 blocks and impenetrable bedrock at level 0. As well as coming out at night, hostile mobs live underground in the darkness, so take care when exploring!

WORLD GENERATION
It may also be useful to know that the Overworld is generated semi-randomly. Each world you create is based on a "seed" which, if reused, will generate the same starter world even on another copy of Minecraft (assuming that it's the same version) with the same biomes and structures in the same places. You can choose to enter your own seed when creating a new world or allow the game to create one for you. If you ever want to restart your world or show the same landscape to a friend, you can generate a world using the same seed!

WEATHER
Most interestingly, the Overworld is the only dimension with weather. Mostly it will be sunny, but it can rain (or, in colder biomes, snow) and sometimes a thunderstorm will generate, with dangerous lightning striking the ground.

Don't worry if it all seems intimidating at first – you'll soon learn how to survive!

Biomes

World generation

BLOCKS

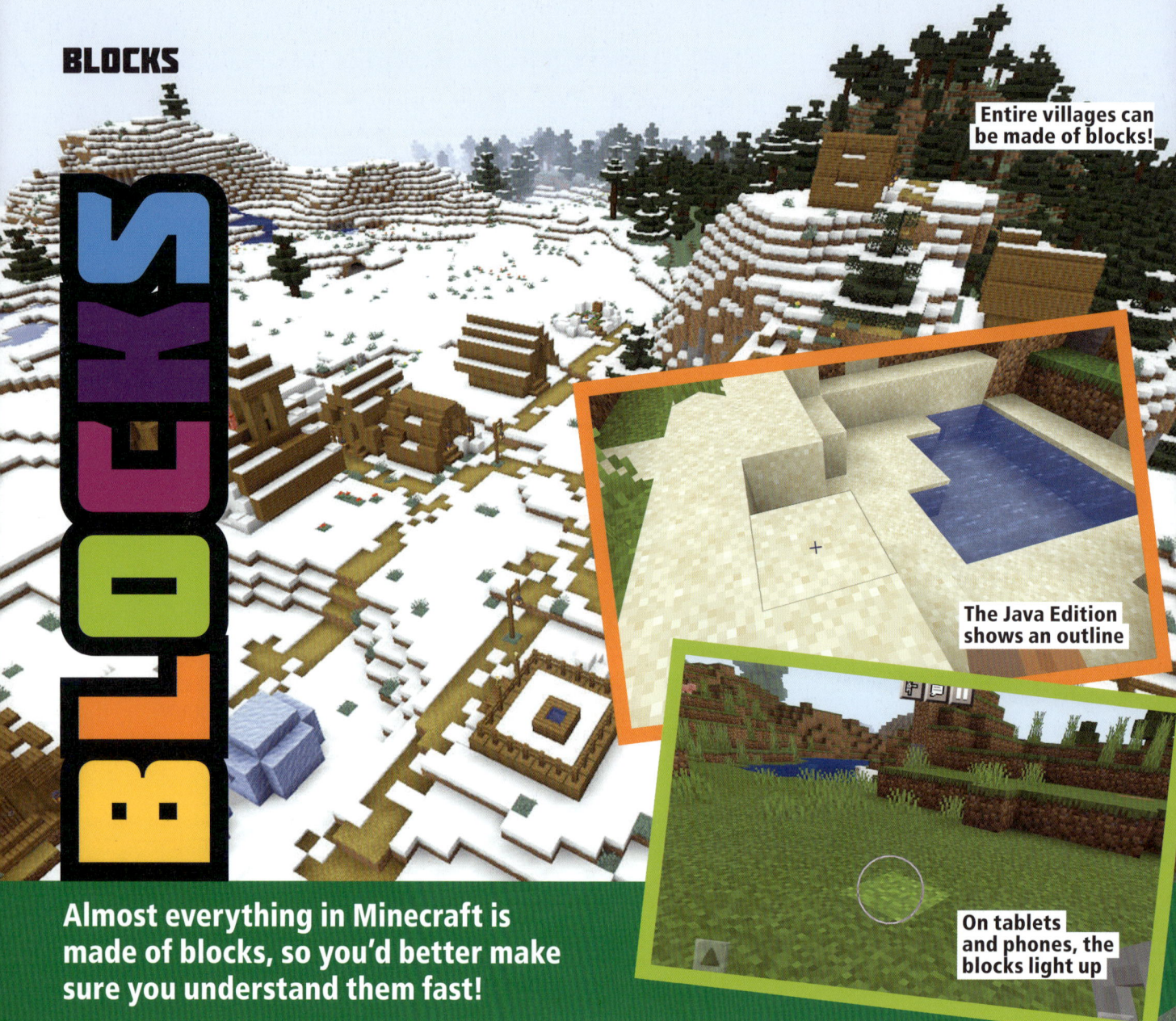

Entire villages can be made of blocks!

The Java Edition shows an outline

On tablets and phones, the blocks light up

Almost everything in Minecraft is made of blocks, so you'd better make sure you understand them fast!

WHAT ARE BLOCKS?
Blocks make up the landscape of Minecraft. The ground is made of stone, dirt and gravel blocks, the ocean is made of water blocks, and even the sky is (technically) made of air blocks! The rough size of a block is one metre cubed, and the player is about 1.6 blocks tall. Anything that isn't an item or a mob is probably a block of some kind.

Blocks can be mined, collected, destroyed, moved – even, in some cases, eaten! They have a huge number of properties, and learning how they interact is essential.

INTERACTING WITH BLOCKS
When you place the central cursor over a block, you'll notice it will become brighter (or get a small outline around it, depending on which version of the game you are playing). This shows you which block is selected – if you use a tool (or your hands), it will act on that block. If you place a new block down, it will connect to that block.

For example, if you want to mine a stone block, you'd select a pickaxe, then walk up to that block. When you're close enough, you'll be able to use the pickaxe on that block, causing it to drop as an item (for example, granite drops granite), drop a different item (stone drops cobblestone) or, in some cases – usually if you're using the wrong tool – get destroyed entirely!

Don't worry about learning everything at this early stage – we will try to explain how all blocks work as we go.

ITEMS

You can carry items in your hand

Your inventory quickbar is always visible

You can equip items from your inventory

Items are the tools of Minecraft – if it's not a block and it isn't alive, then it's probably an item!

WHAT ARE ITEMS?

Items differ from blocks in that you normally carry them, rather than place them in the world. If dropped, an item will float in place on the ground until it gets collected, although if it's left for a long time it might despawn (disappear). Items can be crafted from other blocks or other items, though you may also find them stored in loot chests or item frames.

A huge number of items are valuable and rare, so be on the lookout – learning what you can craft easily and what you should try to collect is an essential skill!

INVENTORY & ITEMS

Items and blocks that you collect are stored in the inventory. You have a few types of inventory.

The quickbar is always visible as you play, and where you store items and blocks that you need to access quickly, such as a sword in case of a fight, or a stack of whatever blocks you're building with. Whichever slot here is selected with a white outline is the item in your hand, which you will "use" if you get close enough to something to do so.

The deeper inventory is accessed by pressing the relevant key or button, and shows items you're carrying, which can be switched in and out of the quickbar. You also have your armour slots, which can only store items you're wearing (more on this later!), and the offhand slot, which is a special extra slot in case you want to carry two items at once or a shield for defence.

CRAFTING

Make a crafting table to craft more items

You have a personal 2x2 crafting grid

Accessing the bigger crafting grid and recipe book

Crafting is one of the basic skills of Minecraft – it's the way you create new items and blocks from stuff you've collected

HOW TO CRAFT
You need to put the items you wish to craft with on a crafting grid. Players have a 2x2 crafting grid for simple creations (like combining coal and a stick to make torches), but you can access a wider 3x3 crafting grid on a crafting table, or use specialised tools such as anvils, brewing stands and more – we'll get to them!

To craft, place the items on the crafting grid. Sometimes they have to be in a particular pattern, but the recipe book, which fills in as you discover new blocks and items, will help. If you can craft something with the inputs you've used, it will appear in the output slot next to the crafting grid. Remember, you haven't crafted it until you remove the item from the output slot!

CRAFTING A PICKAXE
One of the most useful items to craft first is a pickaxe. Here's how to get from nothing to your first tool! First, collect some wood logs by punching them until they break. Place the logs on your crafting grid and you can craft them into planks. Place four planks on your crafting grid (one in each square) and you'll craft a crafting table. Put it down in the world and interact with it to access the larger crafting grid.

Now place two planks in two slots, one above the other, to craft four sticks. Put two sticks back on the grid along with three planks to form the pattern for a pickaxe, and there you go! You've crafted your first tool!

You can make tools with different materials

Blocks get cracks as they break

Some ores need specific tools

MINING

The other core skill in Minecraft – it's in the name, after all! Mining is how you collect blocks and turn some blocks into items

HOW TO MINE

Mining doesn't just mean breaking stone; breaking any block is mining it. You can mine by punching something with your fist, or using a tool like a pickaxe or shovel on it. When you start mining a block, it gradually becomes more cracked until it breaks, at which point it will drop an item, drop itself or disappear. If you stop mining before a block's fully broken, it will reset – you can't partially mine blocks, then come back later.

Blocks are mined at different speeds. You can usually make it quicker using the correct tool. Stone blocks require a pickaxe; dirt, gravel and sand blocks need a shovel; wood blocks need axes; and so on. Sometimes you can't collect a block without using the right tool or material. For example, mining diamond ore with a wood pickaxe will break the block but drop no diamonds, whereas mining with an iron pickaxe (or stronger) will ensure the diamonds drop. Again, you'll need to learn the combinations!

TOOL MATERIALS

Most of the game's main tools can be made of six materials: wood, cobblestone, iron, gold, diamonds and Netherite. Gold breaks blocks the fastest, but has a very low durability. Wood is easy to craft early on, but rarely useful later in the game. Iron is the best all-rounder – most of the tools you use will be crafted from this material. It also has the advantage of being able to break almost anything. Aside from obsidian, iron tools will mine almost any block in the Overworld without destroying it!

SLEEPING

You can sleep at night

Beds reset your spawn point

Get wool from sheep!

When night falls, you want to get into bed – and that's the same in this game too!

SLEEPING BENEFITS
You can only sleep in a bed when it's night time, which in Minecraft's world means when the sun dips fully below the horizon. When you sleep in a (secure) bed, it does two things. The first is that it moves time forward, allowing you to skip the night. The night is when mobs come out, so if you're not looking for a fight it's always worth doing.

The other thing sleeping does is set your spawn point. Even if you don't actually sleep in a bed (because it's day, for example), you can use one to set a spawn point so that, when you die, you appear by the last bed you slept in (as long as it hasn't been moved or destroyed).

You can also sleep in a bed to skip thunderstorms, which is useful for evading mobs and dangerous lightning strikes!

CRAFTING A BED
While it's possible to scavenge a bed from a village house or igloo, they're also easy to craft out of three blocks of wool (collected from sheep) and three planks. The bed will be the same colour as the wool – to change its colour, you can dye the wool or make a white bed, then craft that with dye. You can mix and match planks, but the wool must all be the same colour.

HEALTH

Damage of any kind will lower your health

When you take damage, you flash red

The health and hunger bars

HEALTH

If you want to stay alive, you need to keep your health up!

LOSING/GAINING HEALTH

You can lose health in a number of ways. Being attacked by a hostile mob is an easy way to get hurt, as is falling from a high place onto solid ground. Status effects like poisoning can also deplete your health, as can remaining underwater too long, or catching fire – it's a dangerous world out there! In Hardcore difficulty mode, it's possible to lose health just by not eating enough, and furthermore, if you die in Hardcore, you can never revisit the world to make changes, only to view it – it's best to start on Easy difficulty!

In some modes, your health will automatically regenerate if you're left alone, but normally you'll need to either eat some food or drink a health potion to recover it. Health potions can restore health, but mostly you need to eat food to keep your hunger levels managed. Speaking of which...

HEALTH AMOUNTS

Every mob has a health bar, and that includes you! Your health bar is represented by ten hearts, with each heart representing two points of health. That means you have, in total, 20 health points. When your health reaches zero (all the hearts have turned black), you die and will return to the spawn point, which is either the world spawn (where you started the game), the last bed you slept in, or a respawn anchor (if you've built one in the Nether).

HUNGER

Food replenishes health

The hunger bar (on the right)

You can hunt some mobs for food

Staving off hunger is important for keeping up your performance. Here's what you need to know

THE HUNGER BAR
It might sound like we're in a restaurant, but your hunger is what tells you whether you need to eat food or not. Portrayed as ten meat icons, each one represents two points of hunger. Unlike health, which remains constant until the player takes damage, hunger decreases over time (unless your difficulty is set to Peaceful). Beware – the rate it depletes speeds up if you do things like sprint or jump.

When your hunger drops low enough – below six points – you start to lose health and the ability to sprint. On Easy difficulty, you stop losing health at ten points, on Normal difficulty you stop at one point, but beware – on Hard difficulty you can starve completely to death!

On the plus side, while your hunger bar is filled, you'll naturally regenerate health, which makes it the best way to replenish your health bar.

EATING
Lots of items you find are edible, and you can often craft them into something that restores even more health. Most Overworld biomes have edible mobs in them such as chickens, cows, pigs, sheep and fish. To eat an edible item, simply hold it in your hand and use it. The item will be consumed, and your hunger will refill with a different amount for each item. Cooked meats replenish the most hunger.

SATURATION

All food has a saturation value

Cooked food has higher saturation

You can cook food on a campfire

Saturation is a secret stat, but knowing how to understand it might keep you alive just a little longer!

WHAT IS SATURATION?

In addition to the hunger bar, there's another secret mechanic in the game related to hunger called saturation.

Saturation determines how long your hunger bar stays full until it starts to deplete. As well as replenishing your hunger bar, every piece of food you eat restores a bit of saturation. Knowing how to manage this will mean you can eat less and stay healthy longer, resulting in fewer breaks for food and more fighting, crafting and mining!

When you start, the saturation level is five. Most activities decrease this, and when it reaches zero your hunger bar starts to shudder and slowly deplete. The good news is that saturation depletes very slowly. Swimming reduces it by 0.01 for every block you swim, so you'd have to swim 100 blocks to lose one point of saturation. Breaking a block depletes it by 0.05 per block, so you can break 200 blocks to lose a point!

Sprinting, fighting, being damaged and jumping also reduce saturation – as does having the Hunger effect inflicted on you!

SATURATION VALUES

Generally, complex and rare foods restore a high amount of saturation, and simple, low-quality foods give a low saturation boost. Of all the items in the game, the golden carrot restores the highest saturation (14.4), followed by a cooked steak, cooked porkchop and rabbit stew (12 saturation). The clownfish and pufferfish have the lowest saturation – just 0.2 points.

Saturation is never visible to the player, so you just have to guess whether the food you eat is keeping your energy high or not.

COMBAT

The sword is the main weapon

When you attack a mob, it turns red

Stars mean a critical hit

When push comes to shove, sometimes the only way out of a situation is to fight…

PREPARING FOR COMBAT
Minecraft is full of enemies that want to keep you from living a peaceful life, but you CAN fight back. All you need is a weapon and some armour! When you attack a mob, it flashes red and loses health. Depleting a mob's health will kill it and allow you to collect any items it drops, as well as experience. Of course, the same is true of you, so be careful!

WEAPONS
The main weapon is a sword, which you can craft very early on. Swords are good for fighting up close, though you can also create ranged weapons like bows and crossbows.

If you get attacked when not carrying a weapon, don't worry – other items can be used to deal damage. Axes are a good choice because their sharp edge means they cause more damage than other tools and items. A flint & steel can be used to set enemies on fire, but don't set your stuff alight at the same time!

CRITICAL HITS
A critical hit is more powerful than a normal hit. Learning to make critical hits will make sure fights end quickly. You can make a critical hit with any item, but the sword has the greatest gain from them.

To make a critical hit with a sword or other handheld item, you must first jump. Any hit you make while falling (after you've reached the full height of your jump) will be a critical hit. You'll be able to spot it by the stars that appear when your weapon connects with the enemy, then all you need to do is finish it!

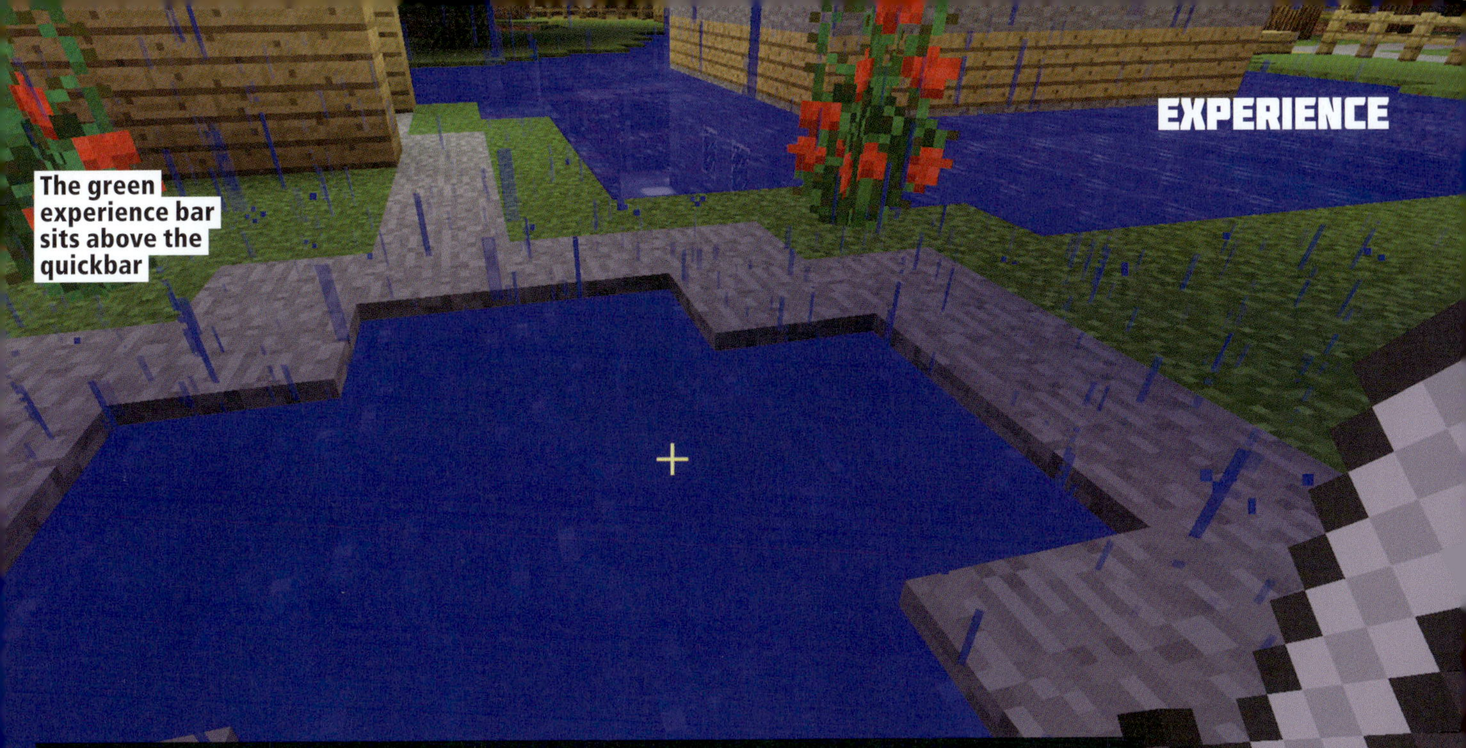

The green experience bar sits above the quickbar

EXPERIENCE

EXPERIENCE

Almost everything you do gives you some chance to collect experience points (EXP), which you can then "spend" on things

You can spend experience on enchanting

WHAT IS EXPERIENCE?
The experience bar, just above the inventory hotbar, starts off empty and fills up with green blocks to indicate your progress to the next experience level. Each level is harder to reach than the next, requiring you to collect more and more experience.

Experience appears in the form of flashing yellow and green orbs, which can be collected by walking closer to them. You'll know you've collected experience when you hear a small chime sound effect.

GETTING EXPERIENCE
The quickest way to get experience is by killing mobs. Target mobs with equipment, as you get one to three points extra per item they're wearing or holding.

You can also collect experience by mining ore (you get more points for rarer ores), smelting blocks into other blocks, breeding friendly mobs, successfully catching things while fishing, trading with villagers – and even for cooking food!

The important thing to remember is that holding onto experience isn't necessarily a good thing – if you die, you'll lose all of the experience collected up until that point, so spend it before you lose it!

SPENDING EXPERIENCE
Unlike in some games, collecting experience in Minecraft doesn't make you any stronger or faster, but it does mean you can do more things. Experience levels are mostly spent when you repair or enchant items. If you don't have enough experience, you may not be able to apply high-level enchantments or repair weapons using an anvil.

Bees

Bat

FRIENDLY MOBS GUIDE

The Overworld is full of friendly (or at least ambivalent) mobs! Here's what you need to know about them all – what they look like, where you can find them, and what they drop

Parrot

FRIENDLY FLYING MOBS

BATS can be found in caves. They have six health, can't fight and drop nothing.
Secret: Between 20th October and 3rd November, they spawn more frequently to celebrate Halloween.

BEES live in nests and hives that generate on trees in forests. They can sting the player if provoked, inflicting Poison. They have ten health and can pollinate crops, speeding their growth.
Secret: Hives must contain five bees for a player to collect honeycomb.

PARROTS live in jungles and can imitate the sounds of hostile mobs. They have six health and drop one to two feathers. They come in five colours – red, blue, green, cyan and grey.
Secret: If music is playing from a nearby jukebox, parrots will perch and dance.

FRIENDLY MOBS GUIDE

Fox

FRIENDLY LAND MOBS

CATS are found in villages and swamp huts. They have ten health and attack rabbits, chickens and baby turtles. They drop string. There are 11 variants, and when tamed they wear a collar which can be dyed.
Secret: During a full moon (in-game), 50% of the cats that spawn will be black.

CHICKENS spawn in grassy biomes. They have four health and when fully grown will lay one egg every five to ten minutes. They drop raw chicken and zero to two feathers.
Secret: Zombies sometimes spawn as chicken jockeys, which is a baby zombie riding a chicken.

COWS drop zero to two leather and one to three raw beef, and can be milked using a bucket. They have ten health and spawn in all grassy biomes.
Secret: Drinking milk removes all status effects from a player, including good ones!

DONKEYS spawn in plains and savanna biomes. They can be equipped with saddles and chests, and drop zero to two leather. Their health varies from 15 to 30 points.
Secret: Donkeys can carry 15 items if equipped with a chest.

FOXES can be found in two places – orange foxes spawn in taigas, and arctic foxes spawn in snowy taigas. At night, they seek out villages. They have ten health, and attack chickens, rabbits, baby turtles and fish.
Secret: Foxes are one of four mobs that sleep – the others are cats, villagers and bats.

Goat

GOATS spawn on mountains and have ten health. They'll charge players and mobs that stand still for too long, doing three to seven damage. They drop raw mutton and can be milked with a bucket.
Secret: If goats hit a solid block, they can drop a goat horn up to twice.

HORSES spawn in plains and savannas, and have 15-30 health points. They can wear saddles and horse armour, and have 35 different colour/pattern combinations. They drop zero to two leather.
Secret: You can make a horse swim behind a boat if you have it on a lead.

Cat

Chicken

Cow

Donkey

Horse

FRIENDLY MOBS GUIDE

LLAMAS spawn in savanna and mountain biomes in four colours. They have 15-30 health and can spit to do one damage. They drop zero to two leather, and can be equipped with chests and carpets.
Secret: Llamas can form trains of up to ten animals if one is placed on a lead.

MOOSHROOMS spawn only in the mushroom plains biome. They have ten health and can be milked with a bucket (for milk) or a bowl (for stew). If you use shears on one, it drops mushrooms and turns into a cow.
Secret: If struck by lightning, red mooshrooms turn into brown mooshrooms.

MULES don't spawn but can be bred from a horse and a donkey. They have 15-30 health and drop zero to two leather. They can be equipped with a chest and saddle.
Secret: As in real life, mules can't breed.

OCELOTS spawn in jungles. They have ten health, and attack chickens and baby turtles only.
Secret: Creepers run away from ocelots (and cats!).

PANDAS live in bamboo jungles. They drop bamboo, and baby pandas can also produce a slimeball when they sneeze.
Secret: A rare variant skin allows brown pandas to spawn.

POLAR BEARS live in icy biomes. They become aggressive if they have a cub, have 30 health and do three to eight damage. They drop raw cod and salmon.
Secret: Polar bears attack foxes that get too close to them.

PIGS spawn in grassy biomes, drop one to three raw porkchops, and can be ridden using a saddle and a carrot on a stick. They have ten health.
Secret: If struck by lightning, a pig turns into a zombified piglin.

RABBITS live in deserts, flower forests, taigas and snowy biomes. Their skin depends on the biome they spawn in. They have three health, and drop zero to one rabbit and raw rabbit.
Secret: One in ten rabbits will drop a rabbit's foot, which can be used to brew a Potion of Leaping.

SHEEP spawn in grassy biomes. They have eight health and drop one wool and one to two raw mutton. Shearing a sheep drops one to three wool, which it can regrow by eating grass.
Secret: Around one in 600 sheep will naturally spawn with pink wool.

WOLVES spawn in packs. If attacked, the entire pack will become hostile. They have eight health when wild and 20 when tamed.
Secret: You can tell a tame wolf's health by how high its tail is.

Wolves

25

FRIENDLY MOBS GUIDE

FRIENDLY SEA & WATER MOBS

AXOLOTLS live in lush caves and come in five colours. They have 14 health and attack other underwater mobs.
Secret: Axolotls die after five minutes outside of water.

COD appear in colder ocean biomes. They have three health and drop one raw cod.
Secret: Cod (and other fish) can be collected in buckets.

DOLPHINS live in all non-frozen oceans. They have ten health and attack guardians. They drop cod, and will lead you to underwater treasure chests if fed raw fish.
Secret: When you swim near a dolphin, you'll gain the Dolphin's Grace speed boost.

PUFFERFISH expand when the player gets nearby. They drop a pufferfish, and inflict the Poison effect for seven seconds when touched.
Secret: Pufferfish can be used to brew the Potion of Water Breathing.

SALMON are found in cold oceans and rivers. They have three health and drop one raw salmon and bone when killed.
Secret: Salmon can swim up waterfalls.

SQUID spawn in ocean and river biomes. They have ten health and drop one to three ink sacs. The glow squid, which spawns in deep places, drops glow ink sacs.
Secret: Squid can swim against currents unaffected.

TROPICAL FISH appear only in warm oceans and have three health. They drop a tropical fish and bone/bone meal.
Secret: Counting all species, colour and pattern variants, there are 3,584 distinct tropical fish!

TURTLES spawn on sandy beaches. They have 30 health and drop zero to two seagrass. When a baby turtle grows into an adult, it drops a scute.
Secret: If killed by lightning, turtles drop a bowl.

Cod

Pufferfish

Turtle

Enderman

HOSTILE MOBS GUIDE

Not all mobs are friendly. Here's a round-up of all of the hostile mobs you might meet in the Overworld – and their secrets

CAVE SPIDERS live in mineshafts. They have 12 health and can do two to three points of damage, inflicting the Poison effect. They drop zero to two string and, rarely, a spider eye.
Secret: In light levels of nine or higher, they're neutral unless already attacking.

CREEPERS are the iconic Minecraft villain! They have 20 health and when they get close they explode, doing 22.5-64.5 damage and destroying blocks. They drop zero to two gunpowder and a random music disc if killed by a skeleton.
Secret: If struck by lightning, a creeper becomes charged up.

ENDERMEN can appear in the Overworld, the End and the Nether. They can teleport and pick up blocks, and become hostile if looked at. They do 4.5 to 10.5 damage and have 40 health. They drop zero to one ender pearl.
Secret: Endermen are injured by water and will avoid entering it.

ENDERMITES sometimes appear when you use an ender pearl to teleport. They have eight health and can do two to three points of damage.
Secret: Endermen will try to kill endermites if they see any.

GUARDIANS spawn in and around ocean monuments. They have 30 health and shoot a laser that does four to nine damage. Touching them also inflicts two to three spike damage. They drop

Creeper

Cave spider

Guardian

28

HOSTILE MOBS GUIDE

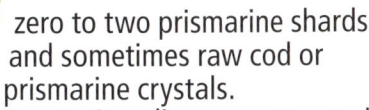
Phantom

Silverfish

Skeleton

Slimes

zero to two prismarine shards and sometimes raw cod or prismarine crystals.
Secret: Guardians are attracted to, and damaged by, conduits.

PHANTOMS are flying mobs that appear at night if you haven't slept for three days in a row. They have 30 health and deal two to nine damage. They drop zero to one phantom membranes.
Secret: Phantoms are undead so can be hurt by Potions of Healing.

SILVERFISH are found in strongholds, igloo basements and mountains. They hide in "infested" stone and stone brick blocks, and attack in groups if disturbed. They have eight health and do one to 1.5 damage each.
Secret: If they escape back into a block, their health is replenished.

SKELETONS have 20 health and drop zero to two bones, zero to two arrows and sometimes their bow. They can do one to five damage per attack.
Secret: On Halloween, they can wear a pumpkin on their head.

SLIMES spawn in swamps and rarely deep underground. When attacked, a large slime splits into medium slimes, and medium slimes into small slimes. Large ones have 16 health, medium ones have four health, and small have one health. They do two to four damage each and drop zero to two slimeballs.
Secret: Small slimes can't hurt the player – their attack strength is zero.

SPIDERS have 16 health and do two to three damage. They drop zero to two string and have a chance to drop a spider eye.
Secret: In the Java Edition, on Hard difficulty, spiders may have one of four status effects: Speed, Strength, Regeneration and Invisibility.

Stray

STRAYS are skeleton variants. In snowy biomes, four in five skeletons will be strays instead. They shoot arrows of Slowness. They have 20 health and do two to five damage.
Secrets: If a skeleton is submerged in powder snow, it turns into a stray.

WARDENS spawn in the deep dark caves. They're blind and will detect your movement, doing 30 damage if disturbed.
Secret: This mob is the tallest in the game – even taller than endermen!

Spider

29

WITCHES spawn in all witch huts as well as in dark areas. They have 26 health and do damage using potions. They drop brewing equipment including bottles, glowstone dust, gunpowder, redstone, spider eyes, sugar and sticks.
Secret: Villagers struck by lightning will transform into witches.

ILLAGERS

EVOKERS are spell-casters found only in woodland mansions and raids. They have 24 health and do four to nine attack damage, as well as summoning vexes. They drop the totem of undying, as well as zero to one emerald.
Secret: If it sees a blue sheep, it will cast a spell to turn it red.

PILLAGERS are crossbow-wielding enemies that appear in raids or as part of pillager patrols. They have 24 health and do two to five damage. If killed, they'll drop zero to two arrows, zero to five emeralds, an enchanted book or iron equipment.
Secret: Pillagers will chase you over long distances.

RAVAGERS are gigantic mobs that appear in pillager raids. They have 100 health points and can do seven to 18 damage from melee attacks. If repelled with a shield, they will emit a roar that does six damage. They can be ridden by pillagers and will drop a saddle when killed.
Secret: They can destroy crops and plant blocks.

VINDICATORS wield an axe and appear in woodland mansions, illager patrols and raids. They have 24 health and do three to 19 points of damage. They drop zero to five emeralds, as well as enchanted books and iron equipment.
Secret: Naming a vindicator "Johnny" with a name tag makes it hostile to all mobs except ghasts and illagers.

VEXES are flying imp-like mobs summoned in groups of three by evokers. They wield a sword, and have 14 health and do 5.5-13.5 damage.
Secret: if summoned by an evoker, they start to take damage after 30-119 seconds.

HOSTILE MOBS GUIDE

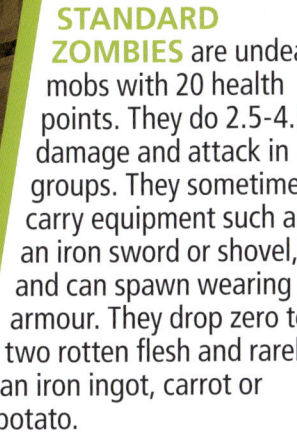
Vex

Drowned

Zombie

Baby zombie

Husk

ZOMBIES

STANDARD ZOMBIES are undead mobs with 20 health points. They do 2.5-4.5 damage and attack in groups. They sometimes carry equipment such as an iron sword or shovel, and can spawn wearing armour. They drop zero to two rotten flesh and rarely an iron ingot, carrot or potato.
  Secret: If they have a helmet or cap on, they won't burn in sunlight.

BABY ZOMBIES make up one in 20 zombie spawns. They're 30% faster than a normal zombie and give more experience when killed. Unlike other baby mobs, they can never grow up.
  Secret: They may spawn riding a chicken. In the Bedrock Edition, they can mount and ride almost any mob, even another zombie!

ZOMBIE VILLAGERS also make up one in 20 zombie spawns. They randomly have the appearance of a villager. They can be cured by feeding them a Potion of Weakness and a golden apple.
  Secret: On higher difficulty levels, villagers that are killed by zombies will turn into zombie villagers.

DROWNED are waterlogged zombies that spawn in oceans and rivers, or if a zombie is underwater for longer than 30 seconds. They're the only source of tridents, which they carry as equipment. They can swim underwater unlike other zombies.
  Secret: If a drowned is on dry land for longer than 30 seconds, it turns into a regular zombie.

HUSKS spawn only in desert biomes, replacing four/five zombies. Zombies that wander in the desert will turn into husks after 30 seconds, and husks that go underwater will turn into zombies after 30 seconds. Their bite inflicts the Hunger status effect
  Secret: Husks don't burn in sunlight.

31

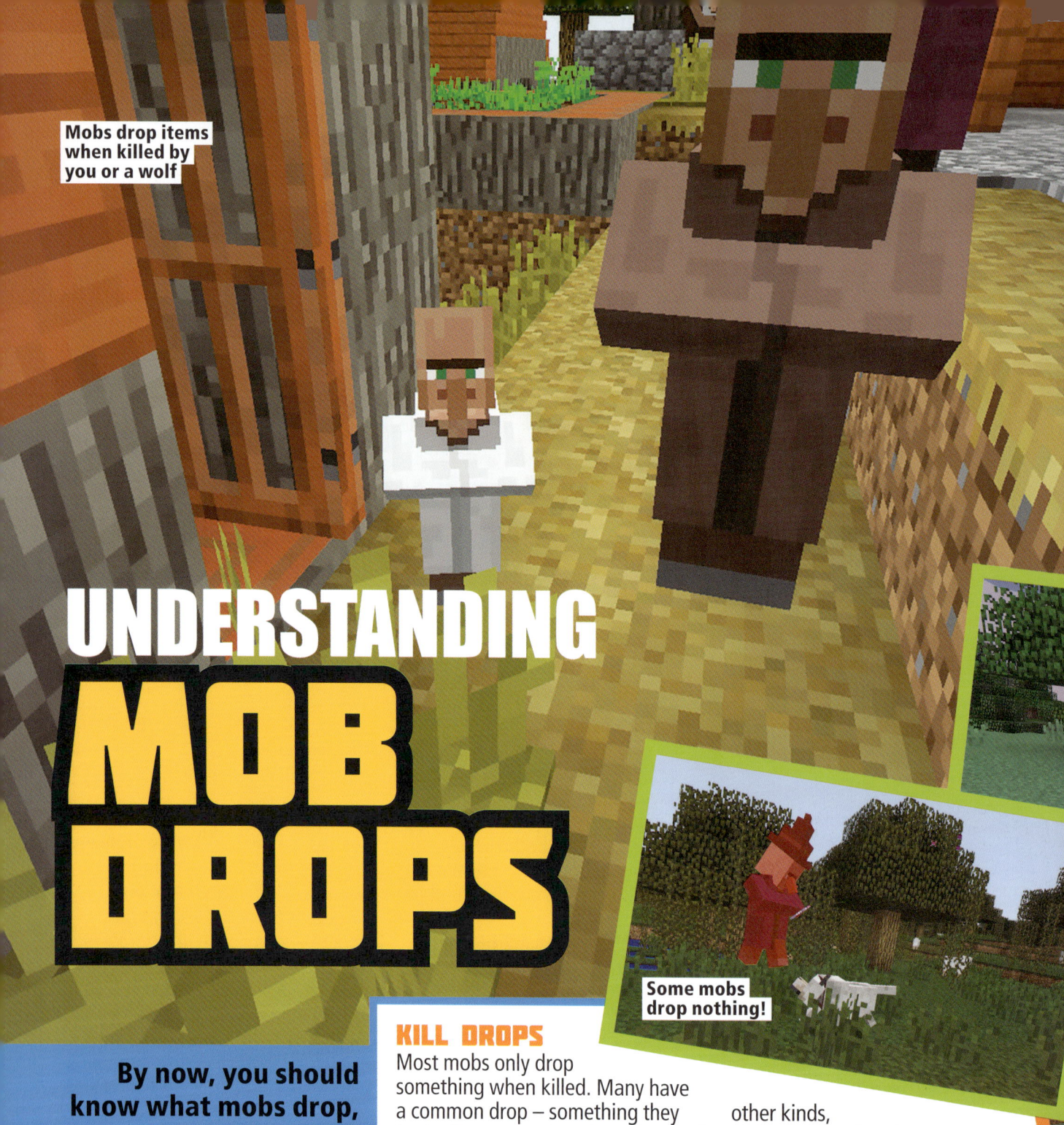

Mobs drop items when killed by you or a wolf

Some mobs drop nothing!

UNDERSTANDING MOB DROPS

By now, you should know what mobs drop, but when do they drop them, and how can you use that to your advantage?

KILL DROPS

Most mobs only drop something when killed. Many have a common drop – something they try to drop every time they die – and a rare drop, which they only drop on occasion. Salmon and cod, for example, drop their raw form every time one is killed, but one in 20 times (or so!) they may also drop a bone or bone meal.

Drops you get from kills are usually more valuable or rarer than other kinds, and you have the advantage of collecting experience as well. However, sometimes it's better to leave the mob alive. If you want wool, for instance, you get more by shearing a sheep than by killing it – partly because the sheep drops less wool when killed, but also because the wool will grow back!

UNDERSTANDING MOB DROPS

Mobs with equipment drop more XP

Some mobs drop stuff without being killed

Mobs may drop their equipment

Players drop their inventory when they die

EXPERIENCE
Even mobs that don't drop items when they die will usually drop experience. The average rate of experience is one to three orbs for killing a tame or friendly mob, and four to seven orbs for killing a hostile mob.

A small amount of mobs don't drop anything when killed, not even experience. Bats and villagers never drop items when they die, not even experience. Friendly baby mobs also never drop anything – we encourage you to leave the next generation of mobs to grow to adulthood in peace!

NON-KILL DROPS
Some mobs drop items when they aren't killed – chickens lay eggs every five to ten minutes, for instance, and cows can be milked for a bucket of milk. Tamed foxes and cats can bring you items after you sleep. Drops like this are perfect for farming items, because you can often repeat the drop without breeding the mob over and over. If you're smart, it's possible to set up a combo of hoppers and dispensers so chickens can be bred from the eggs they lay, ensuring a supply of food.

MOB EQUIPMENT
If a mob is wearing or holding equipment that it spawned with, there's a one in eight chance that the equipment will drop when it dies. This is a good way to get armour and bows early on, when crafting it might be difficult! You also get one to three points of additional experience for killing a mob that's wearing armour, so it's worth seeking them out!

If a mob has collected equipment off the ground, it will always drop it when it dies. This prevents mobs from destroying items they may have collected in error! Endermen that have collected a block will always drop it when they die, which is a good way to collect grass blocks!

PLAYERS
It's worth remembering that YOU are a mob too. When a player dies, they drop all of their experience and everything in their inventory. You can go and collect it if you get there before it despawns – but remember, so can anyone else playing in your world!

Shear sheep instead of killing them!

BASIC TIPS & SECRETS

Now you're familiar with the basics, here are some things to keep in mind to help you become a Minecraft expert!

›› If when you die the bed you last used has been destroyed, moved or buried, you'll reappear at the world spawn – the place you first entered the Overworld.

›› Slimes never spawn during a new moon – if you look up and the moon is entirely dark grey, you'll be safe from them!

›› Hay bales can be fed to horses and llamas to restore health, or placed under a campfire to create a signal fire, with smoke that rises higher.

›› Stairs aren't just useful for decoration or because they're compact – using them also reduces your hunger less than jumping the same distance up or down would.

›› Remember not to kill off ALL the mobs you find. Clearing out a herd makes it harder to get more food later on!

›› Cats and ocelots are immune to fall damage, although they'll still avoid long drops!

›› Shears can be used to collect leaf blocks, plants and wool. They can also be used to shear sheep and mooshrooms, and to disable tripwires.

›› The best fuel for smelting is a lava bucket – it can smelt 100 blocks per bucket.

BASIC TIPS & SECRETS

When you die, you reappear in the last bed you used

Dried kelp works as food AND fuel

Create a signal fire with hay

If you sneak, you won't fall in

To collect honey, you need to use smoke!

» Coal blocks are slightly less efficient than lava buckets, but you can stack 64 in one furnace's fuel slot, allowing you to smelt 5,120 items without refuelling.

» If you jump onto a bed from a great height, you'll bounce on it and only take half of your normal fall damage.

» When sneaking, it's impossible to fall off cliffs, so if in doubt sneak everywhere!

» You can use different wood types in recipes to change the colour or look of some items (such as for doors and boats), though sometimes it doesn't matter (such as in beds).

» Experience is responsible for the "score" you see on screen when you die. The number shown tells you how much experience was collected in total since you last died, including any you spent.

» If you kill a fox while it's holding a totem of undying within its mouth, it will use up the totem's power and come back to life!

» Don't craft everything straight away. Some resources take up less inventory space than their crafted form (i.e. one bone = two bone meal). Leaving them uncrafted lets you carry more.

» After a bee stings something, it will inflict the Poison effect on its target, but then become passive and die soon afterwards.

» You can remove the Poison effect inflicted by bees by drinking a bottle of honey. This will also restore six hunger, but won't remove any other status effects like drinking a bucket of milk does.

» Campfires cook food slower than furnaces (30 seconds vs ten seconds per item), but they're more efficient because you can cook four pieces of food at once!

» Dried kelp is the only item that can be eaten by the player and used as fuel in a furnace – although the kelp has to be in the form of a dried kelp block to work as fuel.

» To collect honey or honeycomb without making bees angry, place a campfire under their nest, and the smoke will calm them.

35

ORE & RESOURCES

Learning to spot Minecraft's valuable ores and resources is a skill you need to learn quickly!

GRAVEL
Gravel generates anywhere stone can be found, but especially in the gravelly mountains biome. Collect it with a shovel – one in ten blocks drops flint (useful for crafting arrows) and the rest can go towards crafting concrete powder (equal parts sand and gravel).

STONE
Abundant throughout the Overworld, stone turns into cobblestone when mined with a pickaxe, which is the main ingredient in many different recipes. Cobblestone can also be smelted back into stone, 20 blocks of which can be sold to mason villagers for an emerald.

SAND
Found on beaches and in deserts, sand can be mined with a shovel and crafted into concrete powder with gravel, or into TNT with gunpowder. You can also smelt it into glass, or craft four blocks of sand into one block of sandstone. Sand is needed to farm cactuses – they won't grow anywhere else.

COAL ORE
Coal is found underground and in cliffsides, and can be mined with a wooden pickaxe or better. It drops one piece of coal per block mined, which is an essential ingredient for creating torches and fuelling furnaces.

IRON ORE
Found in layers zero to 64 of the Overworld, iron ore must be mined with a stone pickaxe or better. The ore can then be smelted into ingots – a useful ingredient in many recipes, but mostly for building durable tools and armour.

GOLD ORE
Rarer than iron (and much prettier!), gold is found in the bottom 34 layers of the Overworld, except in the badlands biome, where gold mines can generate on the surface. Gold ore can only be collected with an iron pickaxe or better, and can then be smelted into shiny ingots.

ORE & RESOURCES

Iron ore

Gold ore

Copper ore

Diamond ore

Emerald ore

COPPER ORE
The latest ore to be added to Minecraft, copper ore works identically to iron ore, except that it can be smelted into copper ingots. Copper ingots make copper blocks, which gradually turn from bronze to green when exposed to air!

DIAMOND ORE
The only bad thing about diamond is how rare it is! Diamonds make very strong armour and tools, but the ore can only be found extremely deep in the Overworld, so it takes a lot of work to get! Make sure you store it as soon as possible once you find some!

EMERALD ORE
The rarest of any type of ore, emerald ore only appears as single blocks, and only in mountain biomes. Emeralds are useful for trading with villagers and have no other unique practical use – though the blocks make nice decoration!

REDSTONE ORE
Redstone ore is found in the same places as diamond ore, but is more common. When mined with an iron pickaxe or better, it drops four to five pieces of redstone dust, which are used for redstone crafting and circuits – but best used for making compasses!

LAPIS LAZULI
Found in layers zero to 34, this drops up to nine pieces of lapis lazuli – useful for making dye or enchantments to take place.

OBSIDIAN
Forms as part of ruined portals or anywhere water flows over lava source blocks (usually deep underground). Obsidian is super-hard, and can be used to craft portals, enchanting tables, ender chests and ultra-secure buildings!

Redstone

Lapis lazuli

Obsidian

Wheat can't be eaten directly

SCAVENGING FOOD

In Minecraft, there IS such a thing as a free lunch – as long as you know where to look for it!

SCAVENGING BASICS
The easiest way to find food is to look for it in and around your spawn point. Different biomes have different types of food available, but there's usually something nearby that you can eat without having to kill anything!

APPLES
If your home biome has oak or dark oak trees, you can break their leaves to collect apples. You only get one apple in every 200 broken leaves, on average, but the apples appear even if the leaves decay, so destroy the tree trunks and wait – if nothing else, you'll collect free sticks and saplings this way! Apples restore four hunger points and 2.4 saturation.

MELONS
In jungle biomes, melons grow in patches, and to eat them all you have to do is break the melon block. It will drop three to seven slices, and each slice restores two hunger points and 1.2 saturation. You can craft a melon slice into melon seeds and plant it in farmland to grow more melons.

SWEET BERRIES
In taiga and snowy taiga biomes, you might find sweet berry bushes. Take care when scavenging the berries because the bushes can injure you, but you can get two hunger points restored and 1.2 saturation from eating each berry you collect. You can also plant sweet berries on any grass to grow a bush, making an easy-to-farm food source.

Apples

Melons

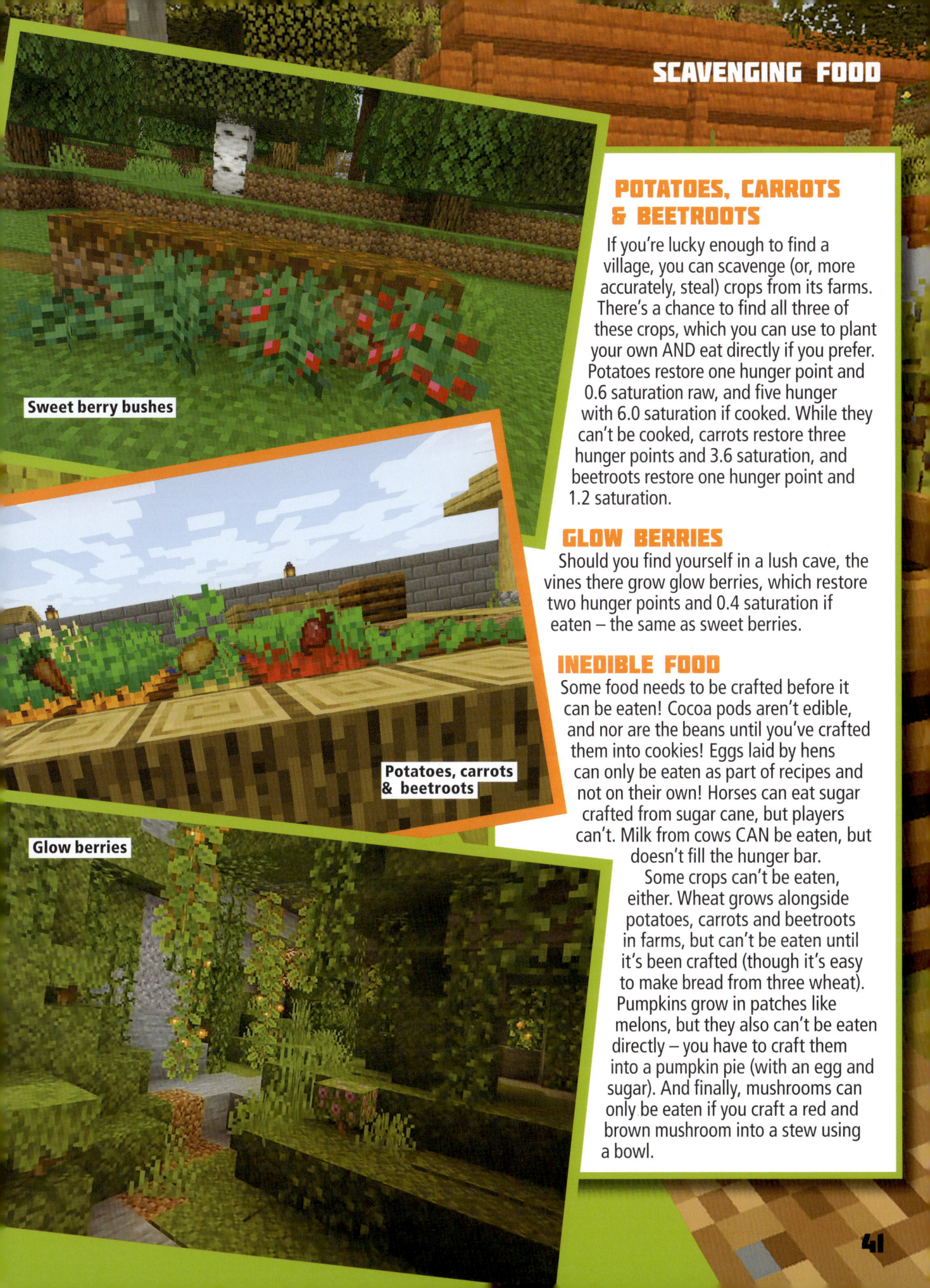

SCAVENGING FOOD

Sweet berry bushes

Potatoes, carrots & beetroots

Glow berries

POTATOES, CARROTS & BEETROOTS

If you're lucky enough to find a village, you can scavenge (or, more accurately, steal) crops from its farms. There's a chance to find all three of these crops, which you can use to plant your own AND eat directly if you prefer. Potatoes restore one hunger point and 0.6 saturation raw, and five hunger with 6.0 saturation if cooked. While they can't be cooked, carrots restore three hunger points and 3.6 saturation, and beetroots restore one hunger point and 1.2 saturation.

GLOW BERRIES

Should you find yourself in a lush cave, the vines there grow glow berries, which restore two hunger points and 0.4 saturation if eaten – the same as sweet berries.

INEDIBLE FOOD

Some food needs to be crafted before it can be eaten! Cocoa pods aren't edible, and nor are the beans until you've crafted them into cookies! Eggs laid by hens can only be eaten as part of recipes and not on their own! Horses can eat sugar crafted from sugar cane, but players can't. Milk from cows CAN be eaten, but doesn't fill the hunger bar.

Some crops can't be eaten, either. Wheat grows alongside potatoes, carrots and beetroots in farms, but can't be eaten until it's been crafted (though it's easy to make bread from three wheat). Pumpkins grow in patches like melons, but they also can't be eaten directly – you have to craft them into a pumpkin pie (with an egg and sugar). And finally, mushrooms can only be eaten if you craft a red and brown mushroom into a stew using a bowl.

41

FARMING

Farmland must be prepped

Eventually, scavenging won't be enough – you'll need to start farming your own food

ESSENTIAL FARMING
To grow crops, you need to find seeds or spare crops that can be replanted. Here are the foods you should look out for:

WHEAT SEEDS: The easiest seed to find, they're dropped when you break wheat – or, more helpfully, long grass. Planted in farmland, they grow into wheat, which can be crafted into other foods.

MELON & PUMPKIN SEEDS: These seeds can be found in some loot chests, but are more typically taken from the fully grown version of the crop found wild in the Overworld. Craft a melon slice or whole pumpkin to get seeds.

CARROTS & POTATOES: Although edible, carrots and potatoes can be planted and grow into crops that drop more of themselves, as long as they're fully grown when you harvest them. The easiest way to get them is to take them from village farms and replant them in your own.

BEETROOT SEEDS: You can find beetroots in village farms too, but they can't be planted directly – when you uproot a fully grown plant it should also drop seeds. You can also get them in some loot chests, and buy them from wandering traders.

FARMING

Melons break into slices

Cocoa beans can be planted on jungle trees

Crops grow in stages

Composters give out fertiliser

OTHER CROPS

COCOA BEANS: Cocoa pods grow on jungle tree logs only. They naturally grow in jungles, and can be replanted on jungle logs in other biomes. Cocoa pods and beans can't be eaten directly, but can be crafted into cookies.

KELP: Kelp grows best in deep water (it only grows upwards into water source blocks), but it grows quickly without needing light, which makes it easy to farm. Kelp leaves can be dried and eaten directly, or crafted into blocks for fuel.

FARMLAND PREPARATION

Once you have crops to plant, you need to create some farmland. Craft a hoe, then use it on dirt (or dirt-like) blocks to turn them into farmland.

If farmland dries out, it will turn back into regular dirt, so make sure there's a water source block within four blocks of it. Moist soil is darker than dry soil, so you'll be able to tell if it's working.

Be careful around farmland – jumping or trampling it can make it turn back into dirt, uprooting any crops planted in that block. This counts for mobs too, so remember to protect your farm with a fence.

CARING FOR CROPS

When you're ready to grow your crop, plant the seeds in the farmland, then leave them. They'll slowly grow into plants through four visible stages until they're ready to harvest.

Crops only grow in a light level of nine or higher, so if you want them to keep growing at night, make sure they're well lit with torches or lamps!

You can also craft bones into bone meal and use it on immature plants to make them instantly advance several stages of growth.

COMPOSTERS

The composter (crafted from seven wood slabs) converts plant and food matter into bone meal, which can be used as fertiliser. Composters have seven levels, and adding material to them has a variable chance of raising the level inside so you can collect bone meal. It takes around 24 small items like seeds or leaves to get bone meal from a composter, around 11 medium items like potatoes, carrots and apples, and just seven large items such as cakes or pumpkins.

TAMING MOBS

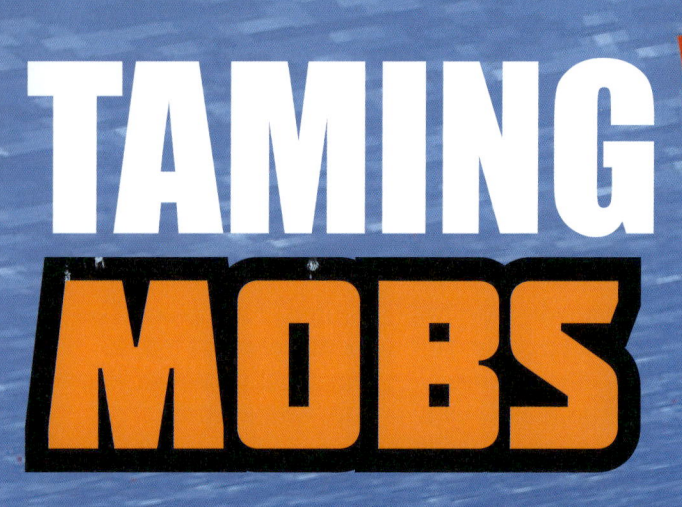

Friendly mobs aren't just a source of meat and items – some of them can be tamed to help you out!

A mob's hearts show when it's friendly

HORSES, DONKEYS & MULES
Taming a horse, donkey or mule can be done easily. First, you have to befriend it by approaching with an empty hand and getting on its back. Initially, it will probably just throw you off. Repeat this enough times, however, and hearts will appear above its head, indicating that it accepts you as a rider. Now you can open the inventory while riding it and equip a saddle, or optionally some armour.

Riding horses lets you move a lot quicker even than sprinting and can allow you to carry extra goods. If you have a donkey or mule, you can also equip it with saddlebags by using a chest on it!

PARROTS
To tame parrots, simply feed them seeds, at which point they'll fly behind you and ride on your shoulder if you stop walking. You can also tell them to perch by clicking on them. There's no real benefit from doing this, but it's fun to have your own flock!

DOLPHINS
You can't permanently tame dolphins, but if you feed them raw cod they'll lead you to nearby shipwrecks or underwater ruins that contain chests, allowing you to collect the loot inside. If you break the chest, they'll lead you to the next closest intact one!

WOLVES
Wolves only spawn in forest and taiga biomes (and their variants). They can be made into tame "dogs" by feeding them bones. Once tamed, the wolf will wear a collar which can be dyed, and becomes breedable – their puppies will also be tame.

TAMING MOBS

You can tame horses, donkeys and mules

Cats can be befriended with fish

LLAMAS
Llamas can be tamed the same way as horses, and once tamed they can be equipped with a chest to carry items and a carpet as decoration. Although you can ride a tamed llama, it's impossible to control its direction. You can, however, attach a lead and walk it around. If you do this, they'll form "trains" of up to ten llamas so you can transport a huge number of items! The amount of items a llama can carry depends on a hidden strength value, but will always be three to 15 inventory slots. If tamed, they'll spit at wolves or any other mobs that attack you.

When you tame a wolf, it gets a collar

Tamed llamas can form caravans

OCELOTS & CATS
These two are very difficult to tame, but it is possible! To gain their trust, hold an uncooked fish and wait for them to approach. Don't move fast or look away as they approach, otherwise you'll spook them!

When the cat gets within three blocks, you can feed it the fish. If it successfully eats, it will become tame two out of three times. Tame ocelots used to turn into cats, but the addition of cats as a separate mob means they'll now simply stop running away from you. Tame cats get a collar just like a tame wolf. Creepers are afraid of cats and ocelots, so having one close by can be useful, and tamed cats will bring a present to you when you sleep – one of a rabbit's foot, rabbit hide, string, rotten flesh, feather, raw chicken or rarely a phantom membrane.

FOXES
Wild foxes can't be tamed, but if you breed a fox by feeding two adults sweet berries, the baby fox will trust you. Foxes that trust you will attack hostile mobs and not run away if you approach.

A baby fox is born tame

Feed potatoes to pigs

BREEDING GUIDE

Whether you're farming items or a food source, or just want your own herd of horses, breeding lets you make it happen

BREEDING MODE
Most friendly mobs can be put into breeding mode, allowing you to turn two animals into a whole herd, given time. To breed mobs, you just need to get two adults in close proximity and feed them the right kind of food. They'll enter breeding mode by showing hearts rising from their heads, then spawn a baby mob, giving you experience points at the same time. It takes five minutes for the adult mobs to recover before they can breed again, and around 20 minutes for the baby mob to grow to adulthood.

HOW TO BREED EVERY MOB
Most mobs need to be fed a certain food to breed, though sometimes other conditions must also be met! Here's how to get each type of breedable mob into breeding mode:

BREEDING GUIDE

Baby mobs are easy to spot!

You can get experience from breeding mobs

BEES: Feed them any kind of flower
CATS: Feed them any kind of raw fish
CHICKENS: Feed them any type of seed, or throw an egg
COWS: Feed them wheat
DONKEYS: Feed tame donkeys a golden apple or golden carrot
FOXES: Feed them sweet berries or glow berries
GOATS: Feed them wheat
HORSES: Feed tame horses a golden apple or golden carrot
LLAMA: Feed them a hay bale (crafted from nine wheat)
MOOSHROOMS: Feed them wheat
PANDAS: Feed them bamboo while they're surrounded by bamboo plants
PIGS: Feed them a carrot, potato or beetroot
RABBITS: Feed them dandelions, carrots or golden carrots
SHEEP: Feed them wheat
TURTLES: Feed them seagrass
WOLVES: Make sure they're tame and have full health, then feed them raw meat

EGGS

Two mobs in Minecraft can hatch from eggs, though both in different ways.

Chicken eggs can be collected and thrown, with each egg that breaks giving a small chance of spawning baby chickens. There's a one in eight chance that a thrown egg will hatch a chick, and a one in 256 chance that it will hatch four chicks!

Turtles lay eggs when they're put into breeding mode. Rather than immediately reproducing, one of the turtles will return to its home beach and lay eggs there on some sand. The eggs will slowly grow until they hatch into new turtles.

BREEDING SECRETS

You can speed up the growth of a baby mob by feeding it the food its species uses to breed. This reduces the remaining time needed to grow by 10%.

Some mobs, such as polar bears, dolphins, parrots, bats and squid, can't be bred by the player, although it IS possible to encounter baby versions of some of these mobs as they can spawn normally.

Since meat is better at lowering hunger than vegetables, it's more efficient to breed and eat cows/chickens than it is to eat the wheat you'd feed them.

Mules can be created by breeding a horse and a donkey, but mules can't breed at all – not even with another mule.

When you breed sheep, the baby will have a mix of its parents' wool colours if the two corresponding dye colours can be mixed. If the parental colours can't be mixed, the baby sheep will randomly take one of its parents' colours.

Throw an egg for a chance to hatch a chick

Zombies try to break turtle eggs

Baby pandas drop slime when they sneeze

47

Iron golems defend their village

Summoning GOLEMS

Golems are utility mobs that you can "summon" by placing blocks in a certain pattern. There are two types of golem in Minecraft: the iron golem and the snow golem

IRON GOLEMS

Iron golems are mainly used for protection – they attack hostile mobs and can also act as an extra target for mobs that might attack you. This gives you more time to counter-attack (or escape!) as you prefer.

Making an iron golem requires four blocks of iron plus one pumpkin. Blocks of iron aren't currently generated anywhere, so you'll have to craft them from iron ingots. You need nine ingots per block, so you'll have to collect or craft 36 ingots in total.

To summon an iron golem, place four iron blocks in a small "T" shape, then a pumpkin (or Jack O'Lantern) on top. The pumpkin has to be placed last! If it's worked, it will instantly become an iron golem. Note that the blocks either side of its "feet" and "head" also have to be empty. Even long grass or a snow layer on the ground can stop an iron golem from spawning properly!

Iron golems are much stronger than snow golems. They have 100 health and four to 31 attack strength. They can't drown and

SUMMONING GOLEMS

The totem for an iron golem

...then build a snowman...

Iron golems have 100 health

aren't hurt by falling, but will suffocate in solid blocks, and can be injured by lava and fire. Iron golems will attack enemy mobs within 16 blocks, except wolves and creepers.

If an iron golem dies, it'll drop three to five ingots and up to two poppies.

SNOW GOLEMS

To make a snow golem, you need two blocks of snow plus one carved pumpkin or Jack O'Lantern.

Blocks of snow are easy to find as long as you're near a snowy biome or a mountain tall enough to have snow on it. Use a spade to dig up a snow layer or two, then craft the snowballs you collect into blocks. You only need eight snowballs to make two blocks.

Getting carved pumpkins is slightly more difficult, but still quite easy. You can grow pumpkins from seeds in treasure chests or find them growing wild. When you have a pumpkin, use a pair of shears on it to carve the face.

To summon a snow golem, place the two blocks of snow on top of one another, then finally the pumpkin (or Jack O'Lantern) on top. It will instantly become a snowman-like snow golem!

Snow golems have low health (four points) and are generally quite weak. They throw snowballs at any hostile mob within ten blocks, which provokes the mob into attacking them, but the snowballs are only actually effective against blazes.

If snow golems enter a hot biome, stand in the rain, or fall into water/lava, they melt. When a snow golem dies, it will drop up to 15 snowballs.

You can use shears to carve the pumpkins off snow golems, revealing the face of a normal snowman.

Collect snow...

...and it will turn into a golem!

Fishing SECRETS

You can collect some fish without a rod

Grab a fishing rod and find yourself some open water – fishing is a relaxing and fun way to get both food AND rare loot

FISHING RODS
You can collect a fishing rod as treasure or by trading, but it's easy to make one with two string and three sticks! A standard rod has 65 durability, and loses one point per successful catch, so they last a while.

HOW TO FISH
You can fish in any still water you find. Cast your rod into the water, then watch the red and white bobber. When it gets pulled down under the surface, reel it in (you have about half a second to act!) and the thing you've caught will fly out of the water towards you.

You get one to three experience points for each successful catch, and the rod loses one durability. If you reel in too early or late, the rod will be undamaged.

Casting a rod onto the ground will cause it to lose two durability points, and hooking a mob will cause it to lose five. You can, however, use a

FISHING SECRETS

Cast off and wait for a bite!

Hooking mobs will damage your rod

Fishing in the rain works more quickly

Boots are a junk catch

Enchanted books are treasure!

fishing rod's lure to set off pressure plates from a distance.

SPEED UP YOUR CATCH
Under normal conditions, it takes 5 to 45 seconds to catch something. The Lure enchantment can reduce this number by five seconds for every level.

If you fish in water that's not exposed to the sky, it takes roughly twice as long to get a bite. If it's raining into the water you're fishing in, the wait time for getting a bite is reduced by about 20%, meaning you can average five catches in the time it normally takes to get four.

WHAT YOU CAN CATCH
There are three things you can catch while fishing: fishes, junk or treasure. If you make 20 successful catches, on average you'll get fish 17 times, junk twice and treasure once.

Of the fish you catch, on average ten to 11 will be cod, four to five will be salmon and two to three will be pufferfish. Clownfish are the rarest: you have to catch more than 50 fish, on average, to get one!

Junk can be any of a bowl, a lily pad, an unenchanted fishing rod, some leather, some leather boots, some rotten flesh, a stick, some string, a water bottle, a bone, an ink sac and a tripwire hook. In jungle biomes, you can also catch cocoa beans and bamboo.

Treasure will be one of an enchanted bow, an enchanted book, an enchanted fishing rod, a name tag, a saddle, or a nautilus shell. You can only catch treasure if the water has open sky above it.

TIPS & SECRETS
The Luck of the Sea enchantment makes it slightly more likely you'll catch treasure instead of junk or fish, but still only by a very small amount!

The rarest item you can catch is another fishing rod. On average, only one in 500 catches will be one! The most common item is the standard fish, which you'll get on average 51 times out of 100 catches.

You get one to six XP points for fishing – it depends on what you catch!

You can trade with any employed villager

TRADING

Trading is another way you can get hold of rare items in Minecraft – here's how!

VILLAGERS

Trading means swapping emeralds with villagers for goods that relate to their profession. There are 15 professions a villager can have, which you'll recognise from their clothing. All but two of these (the unemployed and the nitwit) can be traded with.

Each villager has eight to ten trade slots, with several trading options per slot. Each trade can be made a set number of times before it gets disabled and villagers must return to their workstation to regenerate their trade slot.

EXPERIENCE LEVELS

When you trade with a villager, both the player and villager receive experience, and when the villager has enough experience they'll level up to unlock new trades. There are five experience levels for a villager, represented by a badge colour on their outfit:
- Novice – Level 1 (Stone Badge)
- Apprentice – Level 2 (Iron Badge)
- Journeyman – Level 3 (Gold Badge)
- Expert – Level 4 (Emerald Badge)
- Master – Level 5 (Diamond Badge)

Note that the more times a trade is made with a villager, the more the price of that trade will go up due to demand. The Hero of the Village status effect, which you get by saving the village from a raid, will apply a discount to the prices as long as it doesn't take them below one emerald.

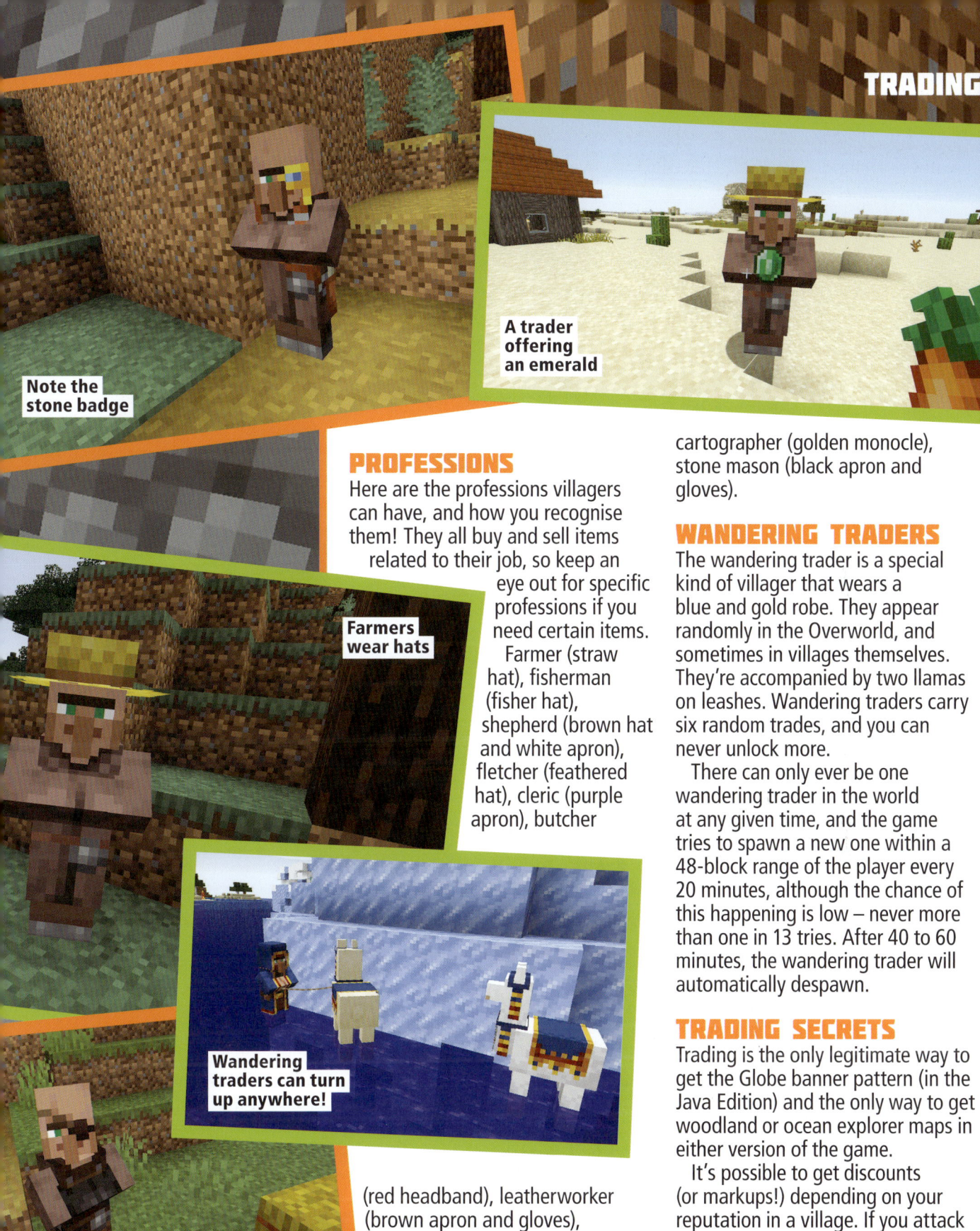

TRADING

Note the stone badge

A trader offering an emerald

Farmers wear hats

Wandering traders can turn up anywhere!

A weaponsmith, recognisable from their eyepatch

PROFESSIONS
Here are the professions villagers can have, and how you recognise them! They all buy and sell items related to their job, so keep an eye out for specific professions if you need certain items. Farmer (straw hat), fisherman (fisher hat), shepherd (brown hat and white apron), fletcher (feathered hat), cleric (purple apron), butcher (red headband), leatherworker (brown apron and gloves), weaponsmith (eyepatch), armourer (welding mask), toolsmith (black apron), librarian (eyeglasses), cartographer (golden monocle), stone mason (black apron and gloves).

WANDERING TRADERS
The wandering trader is a special kind of villager that wears a blue and gold robe. They appear randomly in the Overworld, and sometimes in villages themselves. They're accompanied by two llamas on leashes. Wandering traders carry six random trades, and you can never unlock more.

There can only ever be one wandering trader in the world at any given time, and the game tries to spawn a new one within a 48-block range of the player every 20 minutes, although the chance of this happening is low – never more than one in 13 tries. After 40 to 60 minutes, the wandering trader will automatically despawn.

TRADING SECRETS
Trading is the only legitimate way to get the Globe banner pattern (in the Java Edition) and the only way to get woodland or ocean explorer maps in either version of the game.

It's possible to get discounts (or markups!) depending on your reputation in a village. If you attack or kill villagers, your prices may go up; if you trade with or heal villagers, your reputation goes up.

53

Repairing GEAR

The more you use an item, the closer it gets to breaking

Most tools and armour in Minecraft will eventually break – but you can fix them!

DURABILITY

A tool's durability is normally decided by its material. Wood and gold have low durability, while diamond and Netherite have high durability – a gold pickaxe has 32 durability, an iron one has 250, and a diamond one has 1,561.

Each time you use your tool – to break a block, fire an arrow, light a fire – it reduces the durability by one. If you do non-standard things, like break a block with a sword or hit a mob with an axe, it depletes the durability by two. When durability reaches zero, the item breaks forever – but you CAN stop that happening.

REPAIRS

You can perform simple repairs using a grindstone, found in a weaponsmith's house or crafted from two sticks, a stone slab and any two planks.

If you have two of the same item (such as two diamond pickaxes), you can place them in the input slots of a grindstone. This will combine the two items into one, merging their

REPAIRING GEAR

Combine two worn items for a durability bonus

Repair with a book to enchant an item

Strip enchantments with a grindstone...

...or preserve them with an anvil

Patch an iron sword with iron ingots

durability points and adding a 5% bonus. This bonus means it's worth repairing items instead of just using them until they break! There's no experience cost for repairing items in this way and it has the benefit of freeing up an inventory slot!

Items made of different materials or that are of different types can't be combined. You can repair a stone axe by combining it with another stone axe, but not with a stone sword or iron axe. Note that you also can't "repair" items that have full durability.

ENCHANTMENT STRIPPING

If you put an enchanted item onto a grindstone, its enchantment will be converted into experience and removed. This might be desirable, but usually won't be – take care before you do it! Sadly, you can't remove curses with the grindstone.

ANVILS

To repair items a little more carefully, first craft an anvil. Anvils are crafted from four iron ingots and three iron blocks (31 iron ingots in total).

You can combine two items on an anvil similar to a grindstone, only this method preserves enchantments while costing experience points. Repairs involving high-level or multiple enchantments cost more experience. You can also use anvils to give items a unique name for one experience level cost, or combine similar enchantments to level them up.

You can also use anvils to add enchantments found in books to items. If you "repair" an item with an enchanted book, the book is destroyed and its enchantment is added to the item.

Remember that using an anvil will damage it. They can be used to perform around 24 actions before they themselves break and must be replaced.

PATCHING REPAIRS

If, for example, you don't have a spare diamond pickaxe, but do have a diamond, you can use an anvil to patch the tool. One unit of the relevant resource restores 25% of an item's maximum durability. This can be inefficient – if crafted from scratch, one unit of iron is worth 50% of an iron sword's durability, for instance. That said, it makes sense to patch armour, and can be a useful method of repairing enchanted items without losing them.

Swords are used to attack mobs

Weapon & Armour SECRETS

Learning how to attack and defend yourself is important – but here's the stuff you DON'T know about Minecraft's most useful gear

SWORDS
To perform a critical hit with a sword for extra damage, jump up, then hit the target mob as you're falling down. Critical hits do 150% the damage of an attack (rounded down), but are some of the most powerful strikes in the game.

BOWS
All bows have a durability of 385. The distance an arrow flies depends on how much you draw the bow. At its minimum, an arrow that hits on target will travel one block and do one point of damage. At most, they travel over 100 blocks and do ten points of damage.

CROSSBOWS
Crossbows take longer to load than bows, but are more powerful and more accurate. The least amount of damage they do is six points, and the most is 11. Once the crossbow is fully drawn, you can fire it at any point after. It's even possible to draw a crossbow and deselect it while it's loaded so you can instantly

WEAPON & ARMOUR SECRETS

Use bows to snipe at a distance

Chainmail armour can't be crafted

Tridents can't be crafted

When you wear armour, an armour bar appears

Turtle shells can be used as helmets

fire it when you swap it into your main hand. It's also possible to use firework rockets for a more powerful attack!

TRIDENTS

Tridents aren't craftable, and don't appear as loot or treasure. The only way to obtain one is from a drowned! Unlike most ranged weapons, they don't slow down in water, making them perfect for spearing fish or clearing out drowned. Tridents have 251 durability and lose one point when they hit a mob or are thrown, and do slightly more damage if swung than thrown.

ARMOUR SECRETS

Leather armour has low protection, but can be dyed in a huge variety of colours. Wearing any piece of leather armour will also protect you from freezing if you fall into powder snow.

Turtle shells (crafted from five scutes) can be worn as helmets, giving you the Water Breathing ability, plus protection equal to an iron helmet and durability greater than any armour except diamond and Netherite.

Chestplates provide the most protection per unit of resource, so if you can only craft one piece of armour first, this is the one to go for! Leggings are second best, then helmets, then boots. That said, boots have some of the best enchantments!

Chainmail armour can't be crafted — only found or bought. It provides worse protection than iron armour, but takes higher level enchantments more easily. You can also repair it on an anvil with iron ingots.

Mob heads can be worn in the helmet slot — if you're wearing one, the associated mob will ignore you for 50% of its normal range. Carved pumpkins can be worn to prevent endermen becoming hostile when you look at them. Beware — neither mob heads nor pumpkins offer any armour protection.

It takes 24 units of any particular material to craft a full set of armour. You can smelt unwanted iron and gold items (including weapons and armour) into iron or gold nuggets.

57

JOB SITE BLOCKS

We've already learned about some of the specialised crafting stations that exist – but here's the complete guide!

GET A JOB!
Job site blocks allow unemployed villagers to choose a profession. Some of them are obvious – a cartography table makes a cartographer, for example – but others are less clear, like how a composter makes a farmer. You can collect and craft these blocks for yourself to make crafting and other activities easier, so it's worth learning what they are.

Villagers may also use a job site block to change profession, if their original job site block has disappeared. A villager must visit their job site block to replenish their trades once they've run out of items to sell.

BLAST FURNACE (Armourer)
An upgraded version of the furnace, the blast furnace can't cook foods but smelts ore and metal twice as fast as a normal furnace.

SMOKER (Butcher)
The counterpart to a blast furnace, they cook food items twice as fast as a normal furnace, but can't be used to smelt other items.

CARTOGRAPHY TABLE (Cartographer)
Used to copy and expand maps for less paper (one sheet instead of eight!). They can also be used to lock maps by combining one with a pane of glass. You'll find more details about maps elsewhere in this book!

BREWING STAND (Cleric)
Used to create potions, most of which can't be obtained any other way. Again, there's a whole section about brewing later on in the book!

COMPOSTER (Farmer)
The composter can be filled with organic matter for a chance to create fertilising bone meal.

BARREL (Fisherman)
Contains 27 inventory spaces (the same size as a single chest), but can be placed horizontally or below solid blocks. They're also immune to fire.

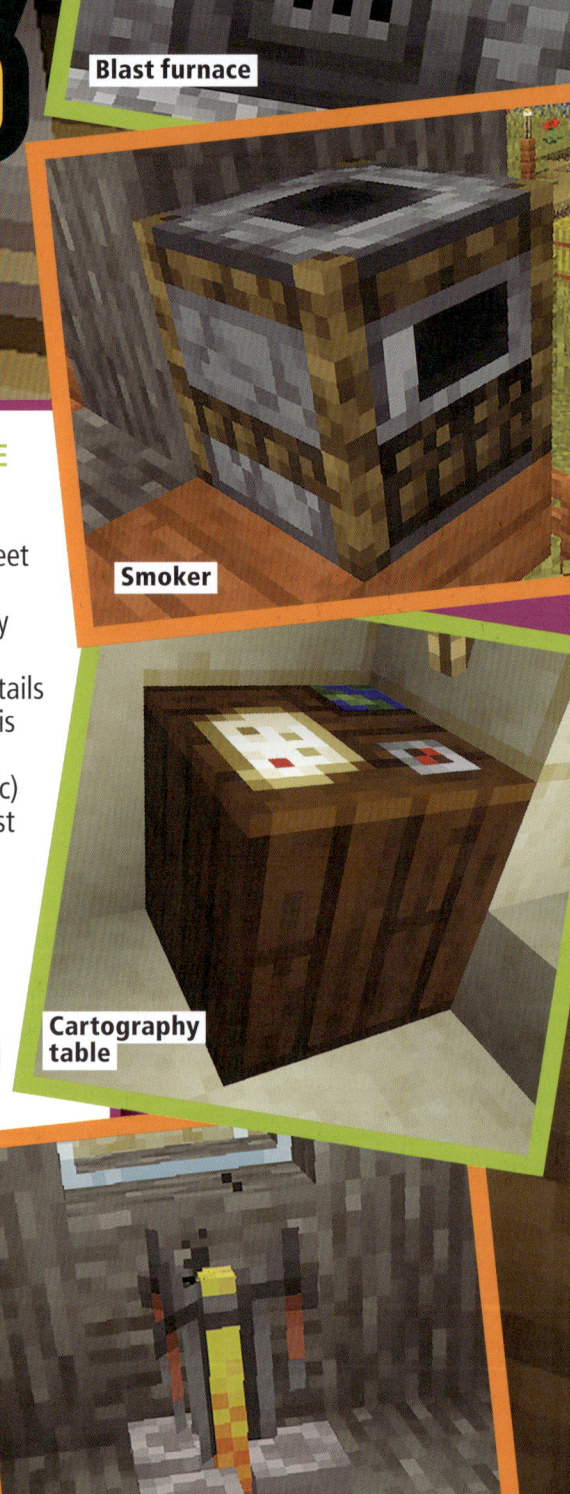

Blast furnace

Smoker

Cartography table

Brewing stand

JOB SITE BLOCKS

FLETCHING TABLE (Fletcher) Currently has no extra functionality, but this is expected to be added in future and will likely be based on upgrading arrows.

CAULDRON (Leatherworker) Can be filled with water, snow or lava. Can be used to fill bottles, remove dye from clothes and banners, and in the Bedrock Edition apply dye to clothes. In Bedrock, it's also possible to add potions to cauldrons for storage and creating potion-tipped arrows.

LECTERN (Librarian) Used to display books in multiplayer modes.

STONECUTTER (Mason) Allows you to craft stone items like stairs and walls more quickly and efficiently – e.g. you can turn one cobblestone block into one cobblestone stairs, whereas on a crafting table it takes six cobblestone to make four stairs.

LOOM (Shepherd) Used to create complex banners, allowing you to apply dyes and patterns to basic coloured banners.

SMITHING TABLE (Toolsmith) You can use a smithing table to apply Netherite collected from the Nether to your diamond items to create ultra-durable Netherite tools and armour. This costs no experience and doesn't remove enchantments from the gear.

GRINDSTONE (Weaponsmith) Used to repair items and remove enchantments in exchange for experience.

You can't hit an enderman with this

Surviving SECRETS

There's always more to learn when it comes to staying alive in Minecraft – but here are some tips we think you should know

>> You can't eat most food when the hunger bar is full. The three foods you CAN eat are chorus fruit, golden apples and milk because they all have beneficial effects other than restoring your hunger bar.

>> Steak and porkchops are the most efficient way to regain health – not least because they stack in your inventory! Rabbit stew and cakes restore more health, but you can only carry one of each in an inventory slot.

>> Crops won't grow when you're asleep, or if you walk too far away from where they're planted.

>> One in every 50 potato plants you harvest will drop a poisonous potato, which is slightly greener than a normal potato and can't be planted or baked. If you eat a poisonous potato, you have a 60% chance (three in five) of getting the Poison effect for four seconds, which will drain three health points.

SURVIVING SECRETS

Cakes are one of the best foods

Crops won't grow when you sleep!

Plant crops in rows

Destroy leaf blocks to get saplings

Dye a sheep for unlimited coloured wool

» If you want to speed up your crop growth, plant them in alternate rows instead of bunching single crops together. Crops grow slower if they're next to lots of crops of the same type.

» You can use anvils and a book to add enchantments to items that they wouldn't normally be able to receive on an enchanting table – adding Sharpness to an axe, for instance.

» For most armour types, boots and helmets are equal, but for chainmail and gold the helmet is slightly better.

» It's impossible to hit an enderman with an arrow fired from a bow or a crossbow – they'll teleport away taking the arrow with them, so don't waste them!

» Doors will keep out mobs but can attract zombies – on harder difficulties, they can even break through wooden doors!

» Although you can see out of windows, mobs won't be able to see in, so use them to plan your moves before exiting your base.

» If you collect a raw ore block (for example, if you use a Silk Touch pickaxe), you don't have to place it then mine it again – you can smelt it into its resource.

» Wood blocks can be used as fuel in furnaces, but it's more efficient to craft them into planks, then burn them.

» Destroying a leaf block drops a sapling one in every 20 times. Jungle leaves only drop a sapling one in every 40 times.

» Resource blocks like iron, gold, emerald, coal and diamond contain nine pieces of their respective resource (i.e. there are nine gold ingots in a block of gold), but they stack in piles of 64, so you can effectively carry 576 ingots/gems in one inventory slot.

» It's always worth adding extra lighting to a village to keep mobs away. You could even build a defensive wall around it if you want to keep the villagers safe!

» Rather than dyeing wool, find a sheep and dye it. This permanently changes the wool colour even after the wool regrows, so you can keep shearing your sheep for an unending supply of coloured wool.

61

62

STRUCTURES & EXPLORATION

VILLAGES

VILLAGES

Every village has a bell

Wandering traders often appear in villages

Villages are small settlements where villagers live, and a great place to find mobs, traders and loot!

LOCATIONS
Villages are only found in plains, savanna, taiga, snowy taiga, snowy tundra and desert biomes. They range from just one or two houses to huge settlements of 20 or more. If large enough, they're protected by an iron golem, while villagers may keep cats, horses, cows and sheep. Remember to check every building – there's bound to be loot around!

VILLAGE POPULARITY
In each village, you have a popularity rating, which starts at zero when you first enter the village. You can raise it to a maximum of ten, or lower it to a minimum of -30. Your popularity level can affect the price of items when trading, and if it drops to -15 or lower the village's iron golem will attack on sight. Trading with a villager will raise your popularity by one point, attacking a villager lowers it by one point, killing a villager lowers it by two points, attacking a villager child lowers it by three points, and killing a villager child or the village's iron golem lowers it by five points.

VILLAGE SECRETS
One in 50 villages will generate as a zombie village, meaning that when you encounter it every inhabitant will already be a zombie!

Wandering traders are more likely to appear near villages.

Many workshops have chests from which you can steal loot. Don't worry, you won't affect your popularity within the village by doing this!

IGLOOS

An igloo!

Pull up the carpet and maybe find a trapdoor

An igloo basement

Found in ice plains and cold taiga biomes, igloos offer a welcome respite from the cold!

INSIDE IGLOOS

Inside every igloo, you'll find a redstone torch (giving off light that won't melt snow!), as well as a furnace, bed and crafting table, plus a rug made out of white and light grey carpet tiles.

The really interesting part is hidden, though, as half of all igloos have a secret basement beneath them. The only way to tell if you've found one of these special igloos is to pull up the carpet and search for the trapdoor. You should find the entrance directly opposite the main door, a couple of spaces away from the back wall. The trapdoor leads to a basement containing a brewing stand, cauldron, chest, priest villager and a zombie villager, plus everything you need to cure the zombie villager, such as a splash Potion of Weakness and a golden apple.

SECRETS

There's no way to tell if an igloo has a basement without visiting it!

Take care if you use the furnace in an igloo, as it's possible for the heat from the furnace to melt the nearby ice block and turn it into a water source block.

The chest of an igloo always contains a golden apple, as well as coal, apple, wheat, gold nuggets, rotten flesh, stone axes and emeralds.

Watch out – like strongholds, the stone brick walls of an igloo's basement can be monster eggs, which contain silverfish!

WITCH HUTS

Witch huts only appear in swamps

The interior of a hut

This hut has spawned connected to a hillside!

As if swamp biomes weren't already difficult enough to survive in, you have to watch out for witch huts too!

APPEARANCE

Witch huts only generate in swamp biomes, both on dry ground and in shallow water. They're usually on tall stilts, and can only be accessed by building your way up to the entrance.

Inside, you'll find a few reasonably uncommon items. You can scavenge a plant pot from the windowsill, which also contains a single red mushroom, and there's always a cauldron inside.

In the Bedrock Edition, the cauldron will contain an amount of a random potion from a list of Swiftness, Slowness, Weakness, Healing, Poison, Water Breathing, Fire Resistance, Night Vision and Harming. Sometimes these potions are splash variants!

SECRETS

Witch huts won't generate in the swamp hills variant of the swamp biome, so you're safe there!

As well as a witch, a single black cat spawns alongside each hut. These never despawn. Additional witches and cats are also likely to spawn in and around the hut. If the difficulty is set to Peaceful, the witch won't spawn with the rest of the hut, but the cat will.

If you spawn a cat with a spawn egg in the area of a witch hut, it will always be black.

RUINS

Warm ruins look like this

Ruins can spawn alone or in groups

Most ruins have treasure to collect

Ruins usually appear underwater and contain ancient, hidden treasures that you can collect – just watch out for drowned lurking in the corners!

LAYOUT
Ruins seem to be the remains of ancient villages. They're made out of sandstone or stone bricks depending on the temperature of the biome they appear in. Quite often, you'll find magma blocks embedded in or around ruins, which suggests some kind of volcanic activity might be the reason they sank! Occasionally, you'll find ruins on or near beaches, but never far from the sea.

You can find ruins in (or at the very edge) of the following biomes: ocean, cold ocean, frozen ocean, warm ocean, lukewarm ocean, deep ocean, deep cold ocean, deep frozen ocean and deep lukewarm ocean.

TREASURE
Most ruins contain a treasure chest that will hold a selection of the following items: coal, wheat, buried treasure maps, enchanted books, enchanted fishing rods, emeralds, leather tunics and golden helmets. They can also contain golden apples and gold nuggets (Java only), and rotten flesh and stone axes (Bedrock only).

Coal and wheat are the most common items found in chests, while golden helmets are the rarest. Finding treasure maps is the best way to get super-cool loot, though. You should find a treasure map for one in every three ruin chests you open, and they'll lead you to much more exciting stuff buried elsewhere in the Overworld!

OCEAN MONUMENTS

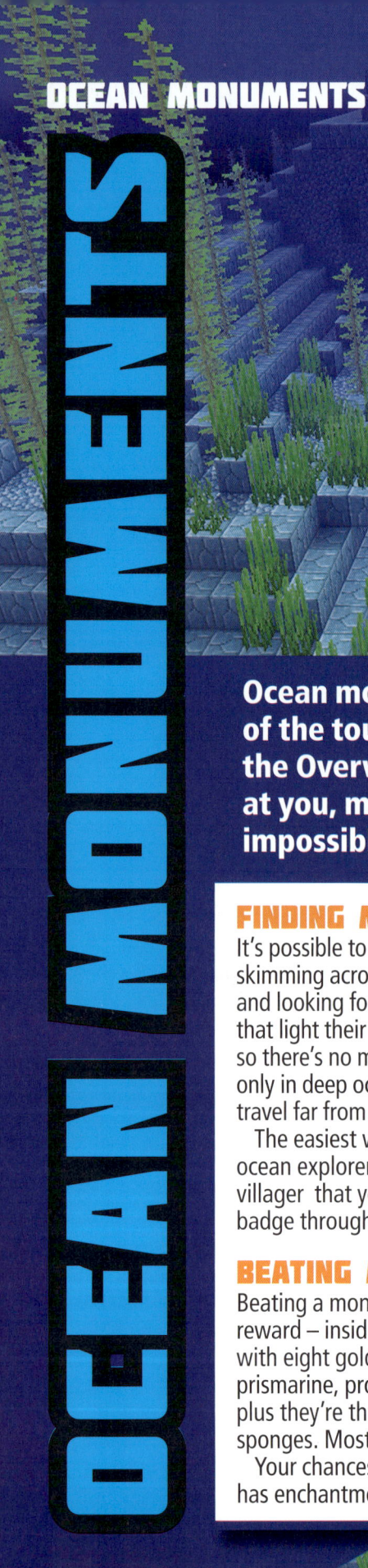

An ocean monument

Guardians

The gold block prize!

Ocean monuments are one of the toughest challenges the Overworld can throw at you, making them impossible to resist!

FINDING MONUMENTS

It's possible to find monuments by skimming across the ocean in a boat and looking for the telltale sea lanterns that light their entrance. These things are huge, so there's no mistaking them! They're found only in deep ocean biomes, so you may have to travel far from the mainland.

The easiest way to find one is to buy an ocean explorer map from a cartographer villager that you've levelled up to their highest badge through frequent trades.

BEATING MONUMENTS

Beating a monument doesn't hold much reward – inside you'll find a treasure chamber with eight gold blocks surrounded by dark prismarine, protected by an elder guardian, plus they're the only place you can find sponges. Mostly, you beat it for the challenge!

Your chances can be improved if your armour has enchantments like Respiration, Aqua Affinity and Depth Strider. A Potion of Water Breathing and a Potion of Speed are good additions too. You receive the Mining Fatigue effect inside monuments, so it's tough to break in or out!

Equipment-wise, bring a turtle helmet and a trident – ideally enchanted. Ender pearls make it easier to get past the guardians at the entrance, but you can't avoid a fight entirely. Axolotls will give the guardians something to shoot at that isn't you!

To make it easier, you may want to build an underwater base nearby. Place a bed in there to reset your spawn point in case you die in the temple, and leave an ender chest inside so it's easy to supply yourself with potions, food and equipment backups in advance.

SHIPWRECKS

Shipwrecks can spawn on land or underwater

Don't forget the loot!

SHIPWRECKS

Dotted around Minecraft, along the coasts and in the oceans, you'll find shipwrecks. And wherever you find shipwrecks, you'll find treasure…

Some boats are more intact than others

SHIPWRECKS

These ruined ships can be almost intact or extremely damaged. They can spawn high up in icebergs, just on land or deep below the ocean, and they might be upright, on their side or upside down.

Inside, you'll find up to three chests with a variety of loot. There are several types of chest themed around maps, valuables or supplies.

Map chests contain buried treasure maps, paper, feathers, books, clocks, compasses and empty maps.

Valuables chests contain iron ingots, iron nuggets, emeralds, lapis lazuli, gold nuggets, gold ingots, bottles o' enchanting and diamonds.

Supplies chests contain suspicious stew, paper, crops (watch out for the poisonous potato!), coal, rotten flesh, gunpowder, enchanted leather armour, bamboo, pumpkins and TNT.

SHIPWRECK SECRETS

Shipwrecks are mostly made out of pre-crafted wooden items, so they're an excellent place to scavenge. You'll find wooden planks, stairs, slabs, doors, trapdoors and fences, as well as logs and chests.

The wood that makes up the ships differs, depending on the type of shipwreck you find, but can be spruce, oak, dark oak and jungle wood.

The best way to find shipwrecks is to watch out for their masts, which often poke above water when they're pointing upright.

Suspicious stew only generates in shipwrecks, so make sure you grab it!

JUNGLE TEMPLES

A jungle temple

JUNGLE TEMPLES

Watch for the levers

Most jungles contain at least one temple, and they're often hard to find because of the thick cover in the forest. But inside you'll find treasures worth risking your life for!

Finally, crack open the chests!

INSIDE THE TEMPLE
Temples have three floors, and are mostly built out of cobblestone and moss stone. A puzzle inside leads to two chests, but you have to get past several traps before you can open them. The chests may contain useful ingots and diamonds, as well as bamboo, saddles, emeralds, enchanted books and horse armour.

Jungle temples are one of the few places where mechanisms generate. As well as a huge amount of rare moss stone, each temple provides you with a free source of redstone dust (15 pieces), tripwire hooks (4), chiselled stone bricks (3), levers (3), sticky pistons (3), dispensers (2) and redstone repeaters (1).

LOOTING THE TREASURE
Getting in and out of a temple safely is tricky, but it can be done. Bring a pair of shears!
■ Enter the temple from the roof and head down to the lowest floor.
■ At the bottom of the stairs, check whether the levers are on your left or right.
■ If the levers are on the left, hit them in this order: right, left, left, right.
■ If the levers are on the right, hit them in the opposite order: left, right, right, left.
■ This will open a secret door revealing the first chest.
■ Keep going, looking out for tripwires. You can use shears to safely disarm them.
■ At the end of the hall, you'll find a second chest with a tripwire directly in front of it.
■ Finally, empty the dispensers for free arrows!

DESERT TEMPLE SECRETS

This temple is half-buried in sand

DESERT TEMPLE SECRETS

Desert temples can be easily seen from far away, although they may be partially buried in sand, which can disguise them!

It looks empty...

...but there's loot down below!

THE MYSTERIOUS PYRAMID
Each pyramid-shaped temple hides four treasure chests, but also an explosive trap, which WILL kill you if you don't take care. The chests will contain enchanted books, saddles, golden apples, ingots, emeralds, diamonds, diamond horse armour, and enchanted golden apples. Most of these things are quite rare, so it's usually worth the risk!

Desert temples also contain a few rare blocks that you might want to bring back with you, such as one blue terracotta and up to 59 blocks of orange terracotta. Temples are also a good source of chiselled sandstone and smooth sandstone, which make great decoration.

EMPTYING THE LOOT
To help you take home the treasures within a desert temple, here's our step-by-step guide to getting in and out of one alive!

■ Desert temples are built on top of a large pit that contains four treasure chests and nine blocks of TNT! The pit is found beneath the block of blue clay at the centre of each temple, as is the pressure pad that sets off the trap.
■ To get down safely, you must dig your way to the bottom. Start at the temple doorway, face the blue clay block and dig a stairway down until you break into the main pit.
■ Quickly place some torches to light the pit. This will stop monsters spawning and setting off the trap.
■ Make your way to the bottom, carefully. Empty the chests, avoiding the pressure plate. When the chests are empty, go back to the surface. Easy!

FINDING FOSSILS

FINDING FOSSILS

Nether fossils are different shapes

Fossils are found embedded in stone

A fully excavated fossil

Fossils are some of the rarest and most intriguing structures, and are incredibly hard to find. If you've never seen one, you're not alone!

LOCATING FOSSILS
Finding fossils in the Overworld is very difficult as they only spawn underground and rarely intersect with caves. You'll have to go digging! The good news is that they only appear in two biomes, so you don't have to search EVERYWHERE – just in deserts and swamps. They always appear a little way beneath the surface – around 15-20 blocks below sea level.

Fossils also appear in the Nether. Nether fossils appear only in the soul sand valley biome, scattered on top of the landscape.

In either case, the smartest thing to look for are the white bone blocks that make up most fossils. They don't generate anywhere else, so if you see one it's definitely part of a fossil!

Unfortunately, as in real life, there are no shortcuts when it comes to fossil hunting. But exploring is half the fun!

COMPOSITION
Overworld fossils are made of bone blocks and coal ore. They're around four to six blocks high and 15 blocks long depending on whether you find a skull or a ribcage. There are four types of skull and four types of ribcage.

Nether fossils are made of just bone blocks – they may be big or small and have strange, twisted shapes that are only small parts of a skeleton. There are 14 shapes in total.

DUNGEONS

DUNGEONS
Just don't hang around too long...

A dungeon has a spawner and chests

They can even be connected to strongholds

One of the oldest parts of Minecraft, dungeons are small but full of loot!

WHAT ARE DUNGEONS?

Dungeons are underground rooms made of cobblestone and mossy cobblestone. They're unlit inside, and contain a monster spawner (which spawns zombies, skeletons or spiders) as well as up to two chests. They vary in size slightly from seven to 11 blocks long.

Dungeons are always connected to caverns (unless a gravel or sand cave-in has sealed up the access point) so you can find them without digging, and while they usually appear close to the surface they can be found at any level of the map as long as you're in a cave. It's technically possible, though rare, for them to appear above sea level in mountain caves. Usually, you'll discover them underground.

Dungeons don't have a roof when they spawn, so if they spawn just below deserts or gravel it's sometimes possible to spot them from where the ground has caved in. Keep an eye out!

LOOT

Their chests contain lots of loot, but most notably two music discs (13 and Cat), which can't be found anywhere else in the game. They can contain many other items, but the most interesting are uncraftable items like saddles, name tags and horse armour (in iron, gold and diamond varieties), and enchanted items like enchanted books and the enchanted golden apple.

Other items you can find include bone, gunpowder, rotten flesh, string, wheat, bread, coal, redstone dust, golden apples, beetroot seeds, melon seeds, pumpkin seeds, iron ingots, buckets and gold ingots.

MANSIONS

Mansions appear in dark forests

Watch out for the vindicator mobs

They're strangely decorated inside

Woodland mansions are huge houses that generate only in the roofed forest biome, and are usually found using an explorer map

LAYOUT

Woodland mansions are semi-randomly generated, so every mansion's internal layout varies. Most have three floors containing a selection of rooms linked to a winding corridor, with a large foyer at the entrance and staircases between each floor. The top floor is always a little smaller than the other two, allowing access to the roof.

Woodland mansions are incredibly dangerous – they're full of evokers and vindicators, in addition to housing the traditional Overworld mobs, such as creepers and skeletons!

If you manage to defeat an evoker, you can collect the ultra-powerful totem of undying, which – if held in your hand – will immediately bring you back to life when you die, saving your inventory from loss. It's also possible to find large amounts of loot and rare blocks in mansions – but you'll have to take care just to stay alive!

WOODLAND MANSION SECRETS

The easiest way to find a woodland mansion is to buy an explorer map from a cartographer villager. If one is nearby, they'll sell you the map you need to find it.

Don't be afraid to break down walls in a mansion – not every room is connected to a corridor, and some never are!

There are 52 types of room, though not all mansions will contain every type of room.

Strongholds are full of mobs...

Throw eyes of ender to locate a stronghold

STRONGHOLDS

Strongholds are huge, maze-like dungeons that spawn underground and contain the only access you have to the End…

...but also loot!

LOCATING STRONGHOLDS

It's very difficult (though not impossible!) to find a stronghold just by luck. The best way is to use an eye of ender, which will literally show you the direction to go to find one.

To craft one, combine an ender pearl (which is dropped when you kill an enderman, or traded with villagers) with blaze powder (which can be created using blaze rods, which are dropped by blazes in the Nether). When you have several eyes of ender, you can start searching.

If you throw an eye of ender, it will move in the direction of the nearest stronghold. You can follow the trail it leaves to recollect the fallen eye, but there's a one in five chance of it shattering! This is why you need lots before you start. Eventually, you'll locate the right spot on the surface to start digging down, which will lead you to the stronghold's entrance.

STRONGHOLD SECRETS

Strongholds are huge and difficult to navigate, so try to mark when you've checked a room – perhaps by putting a torch or other recognisable block on the doorway so you don't get lost!

The most dangerous enemies in strongholds are silverfish, which will spawn and attack you in a group if you destroy an infested block (which just looks like a normal block!).

There's a lot of loot to find, though none of it's unique to strongholds. That said, if you explore the stronghold enough, you'll eventually find the End portal – more on what to do with that later...

RUINED PORTALS

Who built these secret gateways to the Nether, and why?!

A small portal

A large portal

WHAT ARE RUINED PORTALS?

No one can say where they came from, but ruined portals are the wreckage of Nether portals that were presumably built some time in the distant past. They can appear anywhere in the Overworld or the Nether in a variety of sizes and states of disrepair.

There are 13 types of portal in total – ten small and three large. If you wish, you can repair them by filling in the gaps in the frame and replacing the purple, crying obsidian with regular obsidian. At this point, you can use them to travel back and forth between the Overworld and the Nether.

Ruined portals are particularly useful if you get stuck in the Nether without any obsidian – as long as you've got the diamonds to mine obsidian, you should be able to build a functioning portal out of the obsidian in just one or two broken portals.

GEAR AND COMPOSITION

All ruined portals spawn with a loot chest, at least one block of gold, and obsidian, crying obsidian, magma blocks, lava and Netherrack nearby. The rest of the blocks are either stone-based or blackstone-based (in the Nether), except for iron bars (in the Overworld) or chains (in the Nether).

There are many useful items in their loot chests, including a lot of gold items. That said, the rarest are a bell, which can't be obtained anywhere else except from villages, and a fire charge, which can only be obtained by crafting.

ABANDONED MINES

Mines are complicated mazes

They can generate on the surface in badlands

Watch out for loot minecarts

Abandoned mines are usually found deep underground in the Overworld, but in the badlands their entrances can appear on the surface

STRUCTURE
Mines are full of items and enemies, which make them great places to explore and build experience without too much danger.

The start of a mine is a large room with a flat floor covered in dirt and containing up to four exits. There are mineshafts extending out of this room, and more mineshafts leading off those to form a maze.

Mineshafts may intersect with natural caves, so you don't always enter at the "start", and the layout is random, so you never know what you'll find! Staircases and intersections allow you to move up or down a level, but there isn't always any logic to these features.

Mines are filled with common enemies like creepers, zombies and skeletons, but the narrow shafts make it easy to fight them off with a sword or bow. There isn't room for them to dodge your attacks or sneak up!

LOOT
Corridors contain supports made from oak fences and oak wood planks (sometimes lit with torches). Other items you'll find include rail tracks, minecarts, storage minecarts and cave spider spawners surrounded by cobwebs.

Storage minecarts can contain rare items including name tags, beetroot seeds, melon seeds, pumpkin seeds, various kinds of rail, and lapis lazuli.

Mineshafts are great places for collecting rails, but they don't lead anywhere interesting when you find them. Pick up the tracks and reuse them later. Mineshafts are a good source of wooden planks when underground if you need to craft but don't want to return to the surface!

PILLAGER OUTPOSTS

Outposts are full of pillagers

They spawn in any biome with villages

Release the golems!

Pillager outposts are semi-rare structures that generate close to villages and house a large selection of illagers

OUTPOST COMPOSITION

Outposts only generate near villages, 100 to 400 blocks away. They're much larger than most buildings and made of roughly the same blocks that form woodland mansions. They can appear in plains, desert, savanna, taiga, snowy taiga and snowy tundra biomes – the same biomes where villages generate.

As well as a main watchtower, they can include wooden cages containing captured iron golems, logpiles, fake human targets made of straw, pumpkins and fenceposts, and tents made out of wool and fenceposts.

Inside each outpost, you'll find outpost captains, pillagers and vindicator mobs. They also contain a single chest with a variety of loot.

OUTPOST SECRETS

Some outposts are generated in an overgrown state – their cobblestone is mossy and there are vines hanging from it. They're otherwise the same as a normal outpost.

Outposts contain a chest, which can include dark oak logs, crossbows, wheat, bottles o' enchanting, carrots, potatoes, arrows, string, iron ingot sand enchanted books.

The rarest item is the bottle o' enchanting, which drops experience orbs when thrown and only appears in a couple of other places – as treasure in underwater/shipwreck chests and as a purchase from cleric villagers.

Killing an outpost captain will cause the Bad Omen effect to be applied to you!

RAVINES

This ravine formed under a village!

Ravines can even form underwater

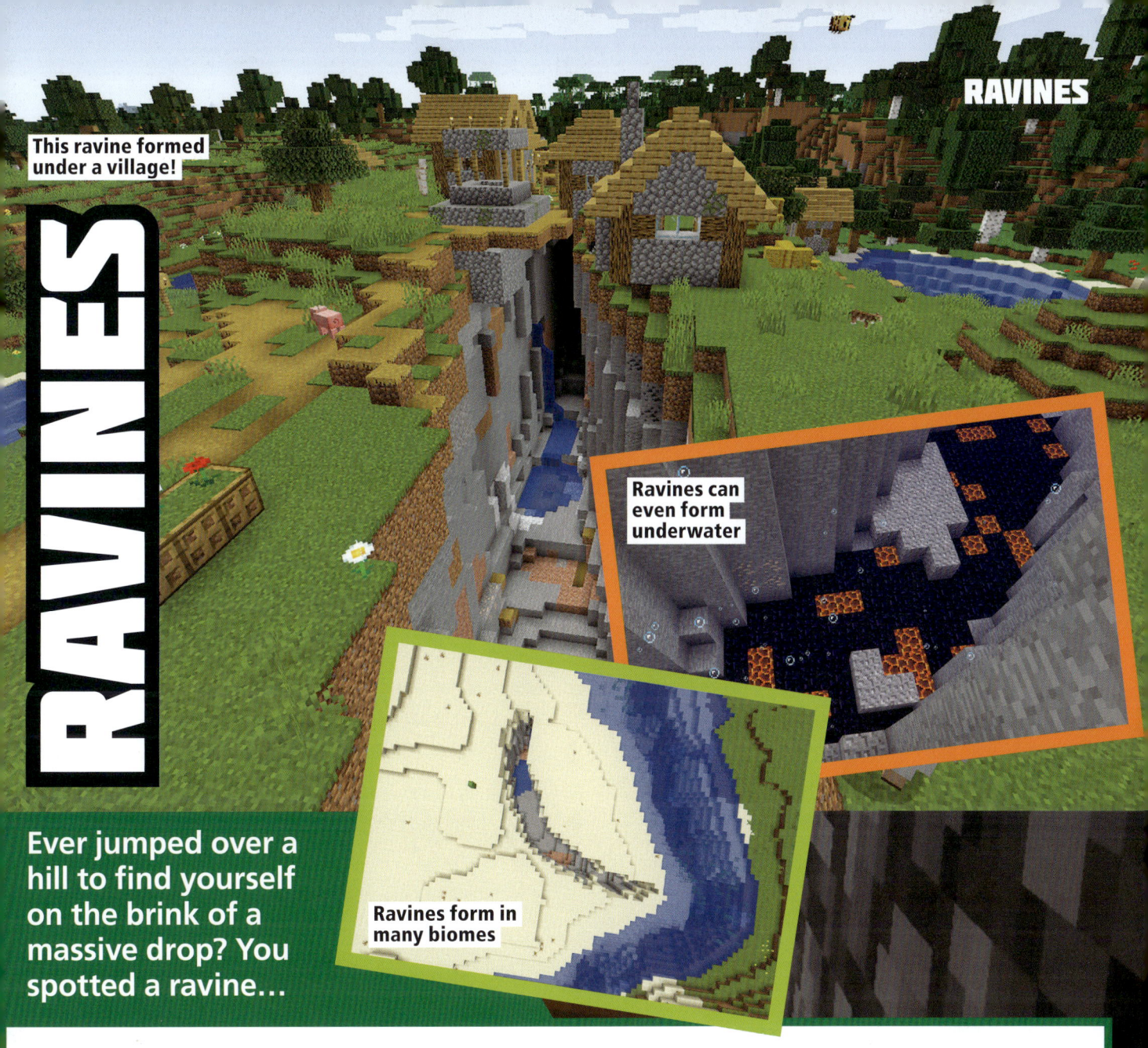

Ravines form in many biomes

Ever jumped over a hill to find yourself on the brink of a massive drop? You spotted a ravine...

WHERE TO FIND RAVINES

Ravines are large, vertical caves that often intersect with the surface, although it's possible for them to form entirely underground, too. They're found naturally in all biomes except for the tundra (ice plains), deserts and mushroom fields. It's even possible for them to form underwater!

Ravines are roughly five blocks wide and can be up to 40 blocks deep. It's possible for multiple ravines to form connected to one another.

TIPS

■ To enter a ravine, the best thing to do is carve steps down one side so you can easily walk up and down, but if you want to do it quickly place a water block on the edge to create a simple water elevator that you can swim up and down.

■ Because of their size and depth, ravines are a great place to look for ore, including rare ores like diamonds. You can see a lot of blocks at great depths without doing much digging, and plenty of good visibility in case of any sneaky mobs.

■ If a mine intersects with a ravine, it will form a wooden walkway, making it easy to spot.

■ Since ravines often intersect with flowing water and lava sources, they can be very good places to find naturally formed obsidian. Always keep an eye out!

■ Ravines are often extremely dark, so remember to light them up to minimise the chance of mobs spawning while you're searching for loot!

You can mark and name areas with banners

Green indicators show a map in a frame

Maps & BANNERS

Mapping the Overworld helps you find and return to the things you discover

CRAFTING A MAP
To make a map, craft a compass (four iron ingots and one redstone dust) and eight pieces of paper (three sugar cane makes three paper). Then surround the compass with the paper on a crafting table. This will create an empty map, which you can start to fill in by looking at it.

When you craft a map, the scale is initially one block to one pixel. Crafting a new map with an existing map in the centre instead of a compass will change the scale the map works on, as if the view has been zoomed out. At the highest zoom level, 16 blocks in the world are represented by one pixel! Remember, you can save paper on this by using a cartography table.

Note you can't zoom out empty maps, so you have to look at every map in between crafting each new version!

MAP INDICATORS
A default map has two main indicators – a white indicator shows your current position. If you place a map into an item frame, its position will be marked on the map (and all

MAPS & BANNERS

Maps show you the local area

Explorer maps show you where cool things are

Put it in your offhand slot to make a minimap

Use a cartography table to copy and lock maps

copies of the map) as a green indicator.

In the Java Edition, you can also place a marker on a map by crafting a banner (six wool and one stick) and placing it in the world, then using the map on it. The base colour of the banner will appear as a small banner symbol on the map, allowing you to remember that something important is there! If you use an anvil to give the banner a name, the same name will appear on the map, meaning you can name locations!

COPYING A MAP
When you've made a map, it's possible to copy it to share with other players. In the Java Edition, you can copy a map by crafting it with one or more empty maps. In the Bedrock Edition, you copy a map by placing it in the first slot of an anvil, and placing an empty map in the second slot. You can also use a cartography table!

FRAMING A MAP
If you put an empty item frame on the wall, you can place a map into it. The map will reach to the borders, so you can tile several maps together seamlessly to form a wall map for showing other players the local area.

LOCKED MAPS
You can lock maps using a cartography table and a pane of glass. Maps that have been locked will no longer update when you explore while holding them, even if the landscape has changed!

EXPLORER MAPS
Explorer maps are special maps that can be bought from cartographer villagers or found in chests and show the location of treasure or structures. Initially showing an outline, they change their zoom level depending on how close you are to the target item, so check them regularly.

MINIMAP
Perhaps the best tip for map usage is if you hold a map in your offhand slot (i.e. the hand you don't use for blocks and tools), it will appear as a minimap in your display, and won't block your view!

A portal without corners

PORTALS

Ruined portals aren't the only way to travel to and from the Nether – you can also make your own

BUILDING A NETHER PORTAL

The minimum requirement for building a Nether portal is ten blocks of obsidian, plus something to light it with – usually a flint and steel. That said, it's worth having at least 20 blocks of obsidian so you've got a way to build a portal back home if you go exploring in the Nether!

Nether portals are built as vertical frames, which must, at the very least, encompass an area two blocks wide and three blocks tall. The frame itself must be four blocks wide and five blocks tall, however they can be much larger than this. The largest possible portal frame is 23 blocks wide and 23 blocks high!

Note that the minimum size portal frame requires 14 blocks to build, however the corners of a portal don't have to be made of obsidian, which is why ten blocks is the minimum you need.

Once you've built a frame, all

PORTALS

An activated Nether portal

You can even ride carts into portals

The largest and smallest portals

You can build a network of portals for fast travel

If you build a return portal from the Nether, a portal spawns

you have to do to activate the portal is set the interior alight using anything that generates fire. A flint and steel is common, but you can also use a fire charge.

When the portal has been lit, all you have to do is step inside the purple swirling energy to get transported to the Nether. Make sure you're prepared – it isn't an easy place to survive in!

PORTAL TIPS & SECRETS

If you create a Nether portal in the Overworld and then use it, the game will automatically create a corresponding exit portal in the Nether. This is also true the other way around.

When Nether portals are created (in the Overworld or Nether), they'll pick the nearest viable location to spawn, which means it's possible for them to appear in unusual locations in the Overworld – on top of trees, or deep underground – but never in places that would be dangerous (i.e. underwater or inside bedrock).

If there's absolutely no place to safely spawn a portal, the game will force the creation of one in the first piece of available space, with four blocks of obsidian either side to act as a platform above potentially dangerous terrain.

Portals can be used by almost any mob, so it's possible to take tame animals into the Nether. But it's possible for mobs to escape the Nether through portals as well.

If you build a portal in the Overworld, zombie pigmen will occasionally spawn around it (unless the difficulty is set to Peaceful).

Note that if too many portals are active in the Overworld compared to the Nether, you might find that they link up in strange ways. It's possible to enter a portal in the Overworld, exit in the Nether, go back into the portal you entered and end up in a completely different area of the Overworld to where you started!

83

Cold biomes
(Ice Spikes)

BIOMES

Almost every Minecraft biome has its own secret – here's a list of (almost) all of the Overworld biomes you'll encounter!

COLD BIOMES
SNOWY TUNDRA Large, freezing cold biomes with only a few trees. Rabbits are the only friendly mob. Villages, igloos and outposts can appear in this biome.
ICE SPIKES Technically a tundra variant, it's full of tall, ice-based structures that can reach up to 50 blocks in height.
SNOWY TAIGA Filled with spruce trees, it spawns the same mobs and structures as snowy tundra, except that spruce trees are abundant and sweet berry bushes can grow here.

TEMPERATE BIOMES
PLAINS Flat, grassy expanses with a little water in, passive mobs are common, including horses and donkeys. You can find both pillager outposts and villages here.
FOREST Packed with birch and oak trees. Variants include the Birch Forest, which only spawns birch trees, and the Tall Birch Forest, which spawns double-height birches.
FLOWER FOREST Despite the name, you won't find many trees

BIOMES

Temperate biomes (Plains)

Temperate biomes (Flower Forest)

Ocean biomes (Frozen)

Warm biomes (Badlands)

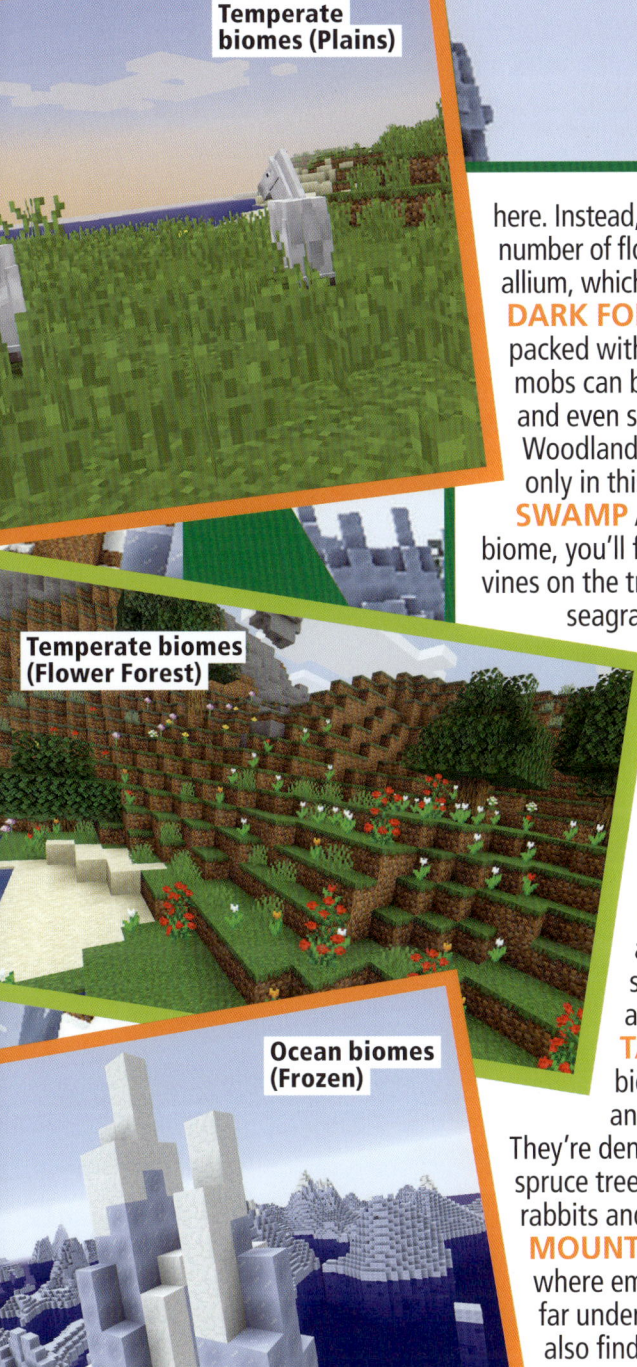

here. Instead, you'll find a huge number of flowers, including the allium, which only grows here.

DARK FOREST Forest so tightly packed with dark oak trees that mobs can be safe from sunlight and even spawn during the day! Woodland mansions generate only in this biome.

SWAMP A low-lying and wet biome, you'll find mushrooms, vines on the trees, and lily pads and seagrass in the water. Slimes and witch huts are found here.

MUSHROOM FIELDS Perhaps the rarest biome, you won't find any mobs here other than mooshrooms. Grass is replaced by mycelium, and both large and small mushrooms are abundant.

TAIGA A large forest biome where villages and outposts can spawn. They're dense with ferns and spruce trees, and spawn wolves, rabbits and sweet berry bushes.

MOUNTAINS Tall biomes where emerald ore is generated far under the surface. You'll also find llamas and goats, and blocks may hide silverfish.

GRAVELLY MOUNTAINS Although called mountains, the peaks here are much less steep and composed almost entirely from gravel.

GIANT TREE TAIGA A variant taiga that contains oversized spruce trees, with a floor made of podzol and coarse dirt, and set with mossy cobblestone boulders.

OCEAN BIOMES

WARM These are the only oceans where you'll find coral reefs, with their coral blocks, coral fans and light-emitting sea pickles.

STANDARD Generate with a gravel sea floor. The Deep Ocean variant is also the only one that contains monuments.

FROZEN Frozen oceans are dark and covered in ice, with large icebergs. Surface ice is made of regular ice, while icebergs are a mix of blue ice, packed ice and snow.

WARM BIOMES

DESERTS Dotted with cacti, they often contain villages, temples and wells. It never rains, zombies spawn as husks, and rabbits are the only friendly mob. Fossils can be found 15-24 blocks below the sand.

SAVANNA Flat and dry, savanna biomes are great places to find horses and llamas. Since cows and sheep also spawn here, they're ideal for farming meat.

SHATTERED SAVANNA The tallest biome. The only thing these peaks are useful for (other than being a good place to start your elytra flight) is coarse dirt.

BADLANDS Large deserts made of red sand/sandstone and terracotta. The only Overworld biome where no friendly mobs spawn. Notable for spawning abandoned goldmines at ground level.

JUNGLE Filled with large trees, you'll find bamboo, vines, melons and cocoa pods growing here, jungle temples, ocelots, pandas and parrots.

85

Structures & Exploration SECRETS

Wandering traders can drink potions

Whether you're poking around Minecraft's pre-made structures or trying to figure out what's out there in the wilderness, you'll find some great secrets, tips and cheats right here

>> A storage room of a woodland mansion contains 42 chests – but don't bother checking them all, they're completely empty!

>> When it reaches dusk, or if they're attacked, wandering traders will drink a Potion of Invisibility so that mobs can't see them. When the sun rises, they drink a bucket of milk to reverse the effects.

>> One great thing about wandering traders is that their trades are random, so it allows you to swap emeralds for rare items that you might otherwise struggle to find!

>> The mountains biome has more caves underground than other biomes do, which makes finding emeralds a little easier!

STRUCTURES & EXPLORATION SECRETS

Mountains have more caves below them

Snow golems melt in deserts

Mycelium spreads to dirt like grass does

Lava lakes can expose ore

Coral can only survive in warm oceans

» Slimes don't spawn close to players, so if you wait around at night you're unlikely to see one.

» If snow golems enter a hot biome (like desert, savanna or the Nether), stand in the rain or fall into water/lava, they melt and will disappear forever.

» If you're sprinting, you can cross a one-block gap without falling or being slowed down.

» Glazed terracotta can naturally appear in underwater ruins, embedded in the floor of some large structures, and in villages.

» Mycelium spreads to other dirt blocks like grass, but podzol does not.

» Take care swinging your pickaxe in an igloo basement – like strongholds, the stone bricks are sometimes silverfish eggs!

» If a village doesn't have an iron golem, it's possible for five villagers to come together and summon one.

» The suspicious stew found in shipwrecks can be crafted by combining a brown mushroom, a red mushroom and any flower in a wooden bowl.

» Eating the suspicious stew will randomly apply one of several status effects from a list that includes Blindness, Jump Boost, Poison, Saturation, Speed and Weakness.

» Lava lakes generate at the same levels as diamond ore, so if you find one carve a border around it and you're almost guaranteed to find diamonds. Make sure you don't slip in!

» Shipwrecks don't all have chests, but if one spawns embedded in the shore it's worth digging it out to see if there's a chest being covered by the sand or dirt.

» Coral will die and turn grey if you remove it from warm water.

» The type of buildings that spawn in a village is random, but some buildings are more likely to spawn in some villages. Libraries are most common in grass plains.

» The "size" of a village (meaning how many villagers it will support) is determined by the number of beds inside the village's limits. You can add extra space for villagers by simply adding some more beds.

87

88

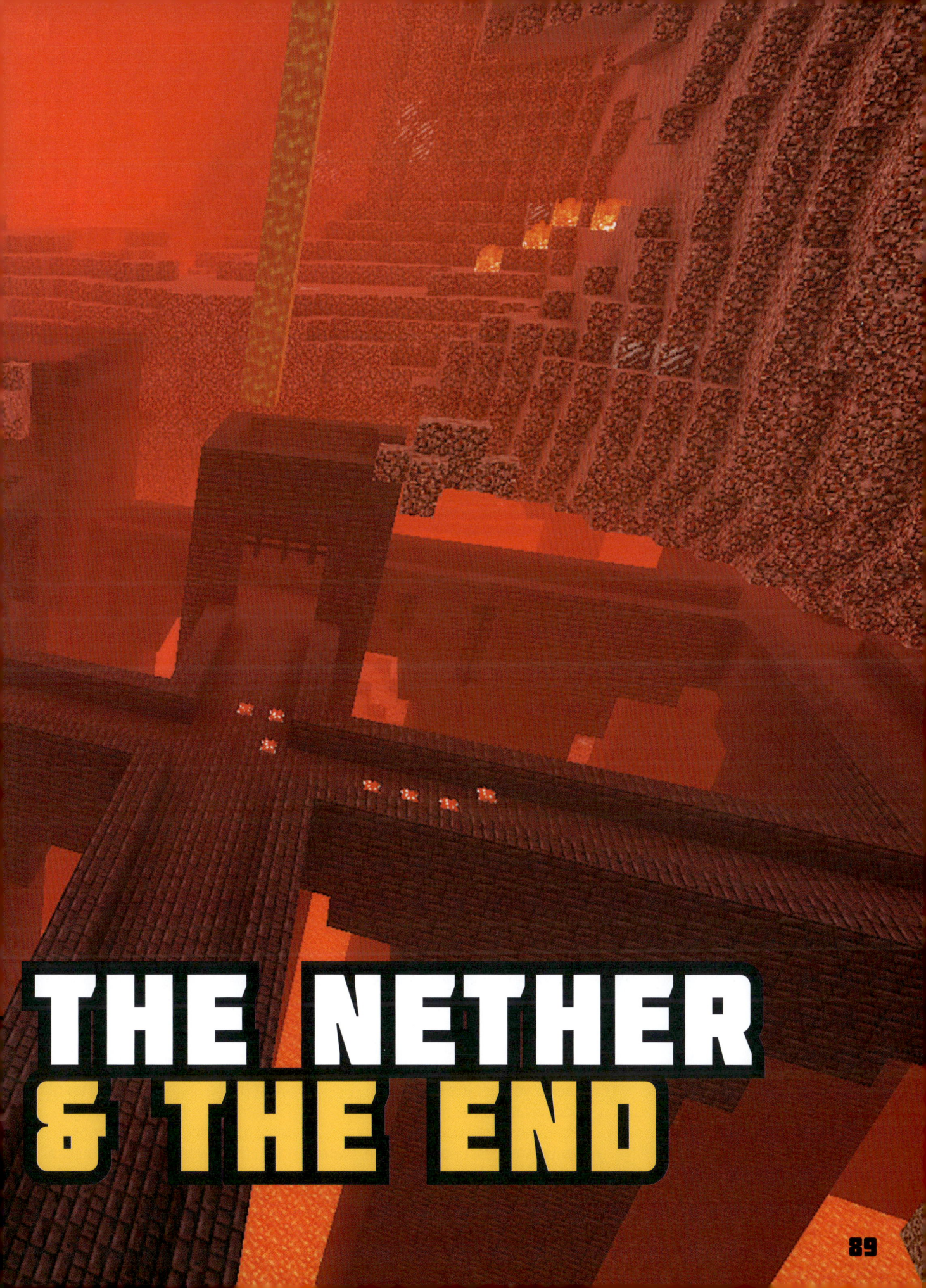

THE NETHER
& THE END

Welcome to the Nether – hope you survive

THE NETHER:
A Need to Know Guide

Step through a portal and you'll find yourself in the Nether. This strange dimension is very different from the Overworld – and a LOT deadlier!

GOING DEEPER
The Nether is the most hostile of Minecraft's three dimensions. Getting there is quite easy, but surviving is a much more difficult task! Before you enter the Nether, make sure you're stocked up on armour and weapons, not to mention the stuff you'll need to get back if you get lost!

Surviving in the Nether is tough, especially if you don't bring your own resources. Food is scarce, water evaporates immediately, wood is difficult to come by, and just crossing the terrain is hard! There are loads of mobs, and while many will leave you alone if you don't attack them, you're just one slip away from being ganged up on!

NETHERRACK
Most of the Nether is made up of Netherrack, a deep-red coloured block that will burn forever once ignited. It's very soft and you can

THE NETHER: A NEED TO KNOW GUIDE

The terrain is mostly Netherrack

There's no night and day in the Nether

Lodestones make compasses work

A respawn anchor

smelt it into bricks for crafting, but it's mostly not much use. Take care when mining it – because it breaks quickly, it's easy to wear down your tools fast or, worse, break open a lava flow.

NIGHT & DAY?!

There's no day/night cycle in the Nether – in fact, it's permanently pretty dark, which is why it's full of mobs. Only the glowstone, lava and fires keep it from being completely unlit. If you think that's disorienting, it gets worse – there's no weather, compasses don't work, spinning rapidly out of control, and even maps produce nothing but a grey fuzz. In case you hadn't realised, things are very different here...

NAVIGATION

Navigating the Nether is mostly a case of keeping track of where you've been using your own markers and landmarks, but if you can get hold of Netherite (more on how later!) you can craft a lodestone. Surround one Netherite ingot with eight chiselled stone bricks to create a lodestone.

Once you've placed a lodestone, you magnetise a compass on it, which makes the compass always point at the lodestone (this works in other dimensions too). If you put the lodestone by your Nether portal, you'll be able to find your way back as long as you're holding the compass!

RESPAWN ANCHORS

When you die in the Nether, you return to your last respawn point, which is normally in the Overworld. You can't use beds here – you can place them, but if you try to use them they explode like TNT! If you want to respawn in the Nether, though, you CAN build a respawn anchor.

To build one, you need at least three glowstone and six crying obsidian. Use them to craft a respawn anchor, then place it at a three-block height from the ground with air beneath it. Charge it up using more glowstone – respawn anchors have five charge levels (including empty), so to activate one the first time you need to use four blocks of glowstone on it. Each block will be consumed as it's used, charging the anchor up to full. When it's fully charged, you can set it as your spawn point, and from then on, any time you die, you'll reappear at the anchor instead of in the Overworld.

Each time you use the anchor, its charge will be reduced by one, so remember to top it up!

NETHER MOBS

Just like its landscape, mobs in the Nether are stronger and scarier than anything you'll find outside it!

BLAZES only spawn in Nether fortresses. They're the only mobs that take damage from snowballs! When killed, they drop zero to one blaze rods. Blazes have 20 health and drop a lot of XP – ten points!

GHASTS have the longest range of all mobs – they can hit you from 100 blocks away. When killed, they drop zero to two gunpowder and zero to one ghast tears. You can hit their fireballs back at them to cause damage, which results in a very powerful explosion. Luckily, they have only ten health!

HOGLINS are animals that attack on sight, tossing you into the air. They have 40 health, and drop two to four porkchops and zero to two leather. They're excellent sources of food! If you bring one to the Overworld or the End, it will turn into a **ZOGLIN**, which only drops rotten flesh.

MAGMA CUBES bounce around and split up when attacked. They have 16 health when large, four when medium, and one when small, and drop zero to one magma cream when killed.

WITHER SKELETONS have a one in 40 chance of dropping their skull when killed by the player. They also inflict the Wither effect! They have 20 health, and drop zero to one coal and zero to two bones.

STRIDERS are the only friendly mob in the Nether. They can walk over lava, have 20 health and drop two to five string. If you use a saddle on a strider, you can lead it around with a warped fungus on a stick (crafted from warped fungus and a fishing rod). You can also breed them using warped fungus. Note that if you take them off lava, they get chilled and move more slowly!

Blaze

Ghast

Hoglin

NETHER MOBS

Magma cube

Strider

Wither skeleton

PIGLINS

Piglins can be found all over the Nether.

ZOMBIE PIGLINS are the most common mob here, although they can spawn in the Overworld near portals, or if lightning strikes a pig. They drop zero to one rotten flesh, zero to one golden nuggets, and around one in 40 will drop a gold ingot.

Because they carry swords, zombie piglins can do a lot of damage. They attack in groups, so the best way to fight them is to climb on a two-block pillar, then strike downwards. The pigmen will surround the pillar, but be unable to climb it, allowing you to pick them off from above.

PIGLINS are hostile mobs that spawn in the Nether wastes and crimson forest biomes. They carry either golden swords or crossbows. Their damage ranges from two to 12 points, and they have 24 health. When killed, they drop zero to two arrows. If you wear gold armour, piglins will become neutral towards you and can be bartered with. If you offer them gold or gold items, they'll respond by offering you an item – throw your item on the ground for them to collect, and they'll do the same in return. Piglins can be made hostile by many things, such as spotting the player opening chests or mining gold ore!

PIGLIN BRUTES are stronger variant piglins found in bastion remnants. They carry golden axes, have 50 health and can do up to 15.5 damage. You get 20 experience points for killing one, though! Unlike piglins, they're not repelled by soul fire. Both piglins and piglin brutes become zombie piglins if taken to the Overworld or the End.

Piglin brute

Piglin

Zoglin

Zombie piglin

93

NETHER BIOMES

Warped Forest

The Nether has five unique biomes, all with their own quirks and secrets – here's what we know about them!

NETHER WASTES are the most common biome, mainly composed of Netherrack, gravel and soul sand. Look out for quartz blocks, Nether gold ore and ancient debris here. You'll also find magma blocks, which burn to walk on! They have huge lava seas, and house both Nether fortresses and bastions.
SOUL SAND VALLEYS are tinted blue and filled with exposed fossils. They're a good place to find ghasts. They're free from lava, and mostly made of soul sand and soul soil. Giant basalt pillars stretch from the floor to the cavern ceilings. You can find both bastions and Nether fortresses in this biome, as well as lots of soul fire and mushrooms of both types.

NETHER BIOMES

Nether Wastes

Soul Sand Valley

Crimson Forest

Basalt Delta

Food is scarce!

CRIMSON FORESTS are red fungal forests where piglins and hoglins reside. The amount of fungus growing here makes them good for collecting food, and shroomlights are a good source of light. They can also house fortresses and bastions. They're great places to find stems, which can be crafted into wood-equivalent planks.

WARPED FORESTS are a denser, blue variant of the Crimson Forest. They're the safest part of the Nether, spawning only striders and occasionally endermen – no openly hostile mobs at all!

BASALT DELTAS are perhaps the most dangerous biome – they're hard to cross because they're uneven and full of lava, as well as home to ghasts and magma cubes. Bastion remnants will never generate here. They're mostly composed of basalt and blackstone.

WATER IN THE NETHER

Water source blocks evaporate immediately if placed in the Nether, which can present a number of problems. Snow golems will start to take damage the second they appear, and wet sponges will instantly become dry sponges. You can still use splash water bottles to extinguish fires, as long as you throw accurately!

The only way you can keep water in the Nether is by putting it inside a cauldron, where it can be used to fill glass bottles or to remove dyes.

FOOD IN THE NETHER

The most common source of food in the Nether is mushrooms. If you bring a wooden bowl, you can craft a mushroom stew out of one red and one brown mushroom. This is perhaps the easiest way to eat, as it doesn't involve any combat.

Killing hoglins is a good way to get meat – the only source of meat in the Nether, in fact! However hoglins are difficult to kill, and the risk of taking more damage to your health than you can regain by eating a porkchop is quite high!

It's virtually impossible to farm conventional crops in the Nether, because even if you bring dirt to make farmland, it's impossible to keep the soil hydrated. You CAN, however, bring herds of animals through. Chickens make an excellent food source – bring some eggs, hatch them in a safe area, and they'll continue to lay eggs, providing a self-replenishing herd of animals. Just don't eat them all at once!

Kill blazes to get rods

NETHER FORTRESSES

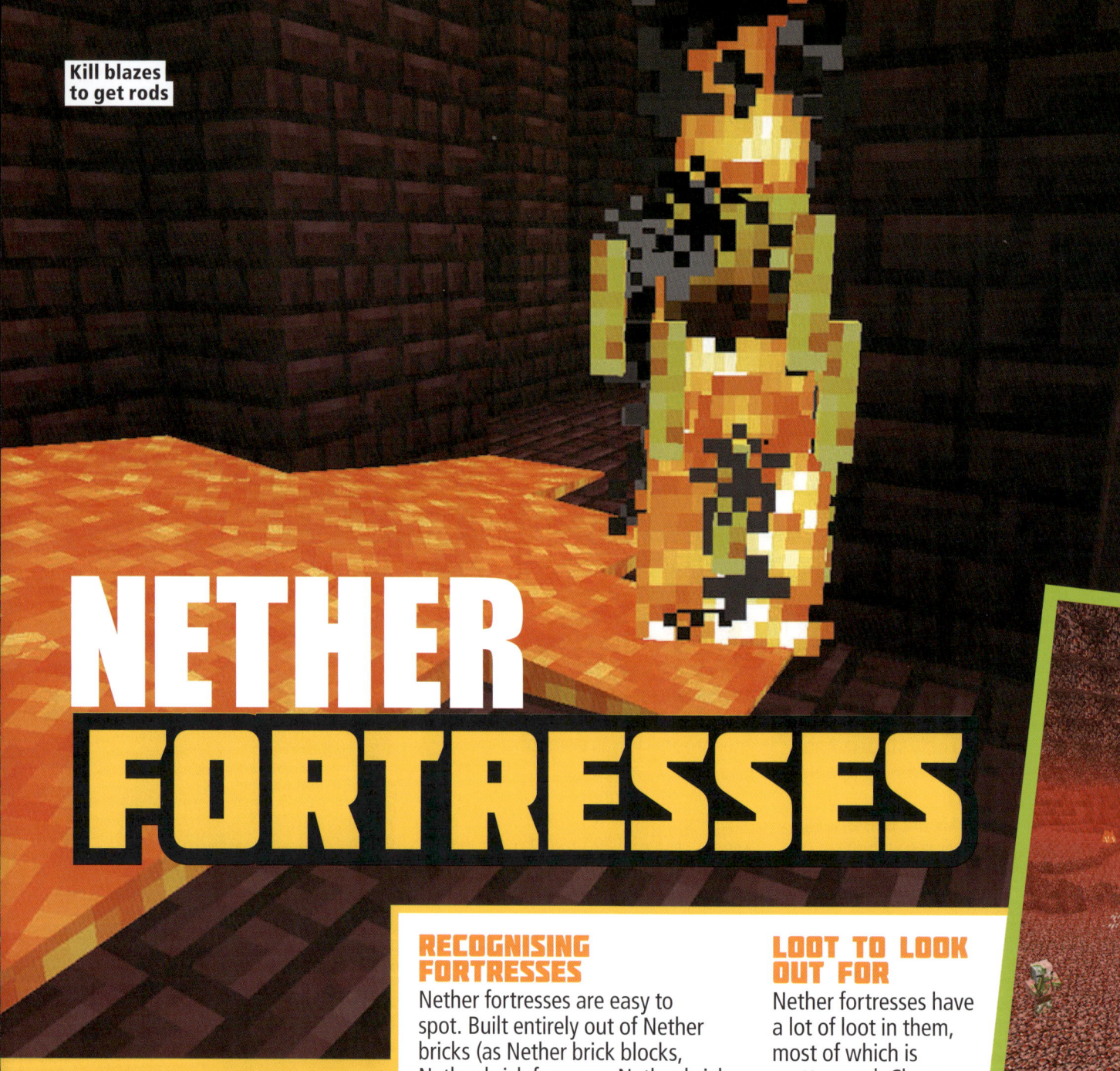

The largest structures in the Nether, and home to some essential gear

RECOGNISING FORTRESSES
Nether fortresses are easy to spot. Built entirely out of Nether bricks (as Nether brick blocks, Nether brick fences or Nether brick stairs), they're composed of long corridors and walkways suspended imposingly high above the floor of the Nether. Often, you'll see their huge support structures set into lava oceans, making them easy to locate! They also carve their way into the Netherrack, creating large tunnel networks. In short, you can't miss them!

LOOT TO LOOK OUT FOR
Nether fortresses have a lot of loot in them, most of which is pretty good. Chests are easy to spot, and the narrow field of vision means it's hard for mobs to sneak up on you – so as long as you're careful, they're pretty easy to explore. One thing to note is that they contain everything you need to build a portal to the Overworld, so they can provide a way back if you lose your original portal.

NETHER FORTRESSES

Nether fortresses are massive and confusing inside

Get Nether wart in fortresses

They appear embedded in Netherrack

Keep an eye out for chests

Set up a portal nearby!

In terms of gear, you can find gold ingots, saddles, golden, iron and diamond horse armour, iron ingots, diamonds, flint & steel tools, golden swords and chestplates, obsidian and Nether wart.

Nether wart also grows in patches in certain rooms of Nether fortresses, planted on soul sand. Don't forget to grab both while you're there – the former comes in useful for brewing and the latter for crafting soul fire torches.

WHY VISIT

In addition to the aforementioned Nether wart, a necessary ingredient for any useful potions, Nether fortresses contain blazes and wither skeletons.

Most fortresses have a blaze spawner, and therefore an unlimited supply of blazes. Blazes, in turn, drop blaze rods, which are impossible to get anywhere else. They can be used to craft brewing stands and End rods, but can also be crafted into blaze powder, which is essential for powering reactions on a brewing stand and for crafting the eyes of ender you need to discover a stronghold. You can also use it to craft magma cream and fire charges.

Wither skeletons, meanwhile, drop skulls you can use to summon a wither, but more on that later...

Basically, if you want to access the more advanced content in Minecraft, a visit to a Nether fortress is essential.

NETHER FORTRESS SECRETS

Ghasts don't spawn in and around Nether fortresses, so you should be mostly safe from them! Zombie pigmen are also rarer in fortresses than outside them.

Mobs spawn faster in fortresses than outside, so you'll never be able to completely clear them for long. Keep moving and bring lots of weapons and armour!

It's worth building a portal close to a fortress when you find one, so it's easy to quickly run in and out to stock up on blaze rods and/or Nether wart.

Watch out for piglins

BASTION REMNANTS

Perhaps the strangest structure in all of Minecraft, these ruined castles in the Nether are a mystery...

BASTION REMNANTS

You can find bastion remnants in all Nether biomes except Basalt Deltas. They're built from blackstone, basalt and quartz, but also contain lots of other blocks – notably blocks of gold and chains, which are rare.

Each bastion potentially contains both piglins and hoglins (if a hoglin stable generates as part of the structure), as well as being the only place you can come across a piglin brute. In treasure rooms, you can encounter a magma cube spawner.

Note that piglin brutes don't respawn once they've been killed, but nor will they despawn on their own!

STRUCTURE & LAYOUT

Every bastion has four types of structure inside it: bridges, hoglin stables, housing units and treasure rooms. These four structures are all huge and connect together in various, sometimes strange, configurations, but you'll learn to recognise them eventually!

Hoglin stables (recognised by the hoglins they house!) contain stable chests, and other housing units may also contain chests. The treasure

BASTION REMNANTS

Bastion remnants are massive and sprawling

Have fun exploring!

They're made of blackstone

There are several types of room

Look out for loot chests

room, guarded by a magma cube, contains blocks of gold and two treasure chests, which have unique loot in them.

It's possible for parts of bastions to spawn embedded inside the Netherrack, although most of the structure is likely to be visible because they're so huge!

As with Nether fortresses, if you find a bastion it makes sense to place a portal nearby before you start exploring. These things are tough to do in one go!

BASTION LOOT

Chests in three of the four sections of a bastion can contain items drawn from their own pool of loot: BASTION BRIDGE CHESTS contain lodestones, arrows, iron and gold in various forms, string, leather, crying obsidian, crossbows, and enchanted golden tools and armour. HOGLIN STABLE CHESTS contain food in the form of both raw and cooked porkchops, and golden apples and carrots. They also contain Netherite scrap and ancient debris, saddles, diamond pickaxes and shovels, leather, crying obsidian, and more common items like soul sand, string, arrows and crimson fungus.

TREASURE CHESTS are the most valuable loot chests in the Nether. As well as containing both pre-made Netherite ingots and ancient debris, they can contain spectral arrows, gold and iron blocks and ingots, magma cream, crying obsidian and diamond equipment of all kinds – some of which is already enchanted.

You can also encounter the generic bastion chest in all sections of a bastion, which contain arrows, magma cream, iron and gold in various forms, enchanted books, golden items, crossbows, Netherite scrap and ancient debris, crying obsidian and arrows.

UNIQUE ITEMS

The generic chest type can also contain two items that can't be found anywhere else. The first is PIGSTEP, the Nether's only music disc! The record is red, rather than black, and is made by a different composer to the other discs.

The second is the SNOUT BANNER PATTERN, a loom pattern to create a pig snout in the centre of a banner.

Netherite floats in lava

NETHERITE GEAR

It's the Nether's most valuable resource – but what is Netherite, and what's it for?

A Netherite sword

WHAT IS NETHERITE?

Netherite is a form of metal found only in the Nether. You can craft it by digging around the Nether to find ancient debris. This can be smelted into Netherite scrap, which you can craft with gold to create Netherite ingots.

Netherite items have special properties – they float in lava, can't be destroyed by fire, and are more durable than diamond. The armour also has its own unique appearance compared to other forms of armour. No wonder it's so sought after!

Netherite blocks are as blast resistant as obsidian, but can also be pushed with pistons. Like other resource blocks, it's crafted from nine of its component material – in this case, nine Netherite ingots – and can be crafted back into nine ingots too.

NETHERITE GEAR

Ancient debris and Netherite scrap

A full set of Netherite armour!

Netherite is found underground in the Nether

The strongest hoe ever

FINDING ANCIENT DEBRIS

The ore form of Netherite scrap is found in mineral veins in the Nether. Unlike most mineral veins, ancient debris never generates exposed to air, meaning you have to mine to find it. It only generates in bunches of one to three blocks, so you won't find a lot very easily. Ancient debris drops as an item if mined with a diamond pickaxe, and simply breaks, dropping nothing, if mined with any other tool.

Smelting ancient debris into Netherite scrap nets you two experience points – the highest from any act of smelting!

CRAFTING WITH NETHERITE

As well as being the centre of a lodestone, Netherite ingots can be used to upgrade diamond gear on a smithing table. Rather than crafting items directly from Netherite ingots, you augment diamond gear with just a single ingot.

NETHERITE SWORDS and NETHERITE AXES do a point more damage than their diamond counterparts and have a durability of 2031 – 25% more. The axe is also slightly faster than diamond, but still not as fast as gold.

NETHERITE PICKAXES, SHOVELS and HOES are also slightly faster than their counterparts with the same high durability.

Netherite can also be used to craft and power beacons, as discussed later in this book!

NETHERITE ARMOUR

Netherite armour encompasses four pieces – helmet, chestplate, leggings and boots – although they look more fearsome! Netherite helmets add three protection and have a durability of 407. Netherite chestplates add eight protection and have a durability of 592. Netherite leggings add six protection and have a durability of 555. Netherite boots add three protection and have a durability of 481.

In all cases, Netherite armour gives as much protection as the diamond version, but it also looks much cooler and has a higher durability – so if you're looking for that extra edge in combat, it's definitely worth getting!

Remember, because Netherite gear only needs one ingot to be created regardless of what you're crafting, you should get the best value by starting with chestplates, then leggings, then boots, then helmets.

Get blaze rods to make blaze powder

Reaching
THE END

How do you get to the End? Follow these simple steps!

The End is the third and final dimension in the Minecraft world. It's the home of the ender dragon, and a place where you can find all sorts of rare and weird things. Beating the ender dragon is the game's main challenge, but once you've done that, the End has a lot more to discover.

Here's everything you have to do in order to reach the End and give yourself a chance of winning!

>> Start the game. Build a shelter, and craft yourself some decent armour and tools. Each night, go out and kill mobs, looking particularly for endermen. You need to collect as many ender pearls as you can, but 64 should be more than enough to get you experience and reach the End.

>> Collect enough diamonds to craft a diamond pickaxe. You can mine for diamond ore, search treasure chests or make trades. You only need three, but the more you collect, the better the armour and weapons you can craft.

>> Use the diamond pickaxe to mine obsidian and make a Nether portal. You need at least ten blocks.

REACHING THE END

Start by killing endermen

Build a Nether portal

Look for the stronghold portal room

Fill the frame with eyes of ender

And prepare to fight the dragon!

›› Ignite your portal (a flint and steel is best for this) and enter the Nether. You don't HAVE to enchant your weapons and armour, but you probably should get used to it. It will be tough to beat the dragon with just your standard gear.

›› Find a Nether fortress in the Nether. You need to kill blazes – the yellow flying mobs – and collect the blaze rods they drop. Again, collect as many as possible.

›› Return to the Overworld, and craft your blaze rods into blaze powder.

›› Combine the blaze powder with ender pearls to create as many eyes of ender as you can. The absolute minimum you need is 11, but that assumes nothing goes wrong – don't continue until you have at least double that amount, and ideally even more!

›› Throw your eyes of ender and follow them to the nearest stronghold. Make sure you have at least 11 intact when you enter the stronghold, and don't lose any on the way!

›› Explore the stronghold until you find the End portal room. If you can't find an End portal in the stronghold, look for a different stronghold and try again – sometimes they get destroyed when caves generate!

›› Fill the portal frame with eyes of ender. A portal needs 12 eyes in total to activate (there should be at least one in there already).

›› You can now enter the End, but before you do load up on the strongest armour and weapons possible. If you can, bring some friends to go with you! The fight you're about to have isn't easy. Make sure you take a good bow!

›› When you're ready, you can enter the portal to the End. Only do so when you're DEFINITELY prepared, because once you go in, the only way to get back is to defeat the ender dragon – or die trying!

Shulkers fire anti-gravity bullets at you

THE END –
A Need to Know Guide

Minecraft's third and final dimension is one of danger and mystery – and it is very different from the others!

TERRAIN
When you enter the End, you'll have to defeat the ender dragon before you can proceed – but once the dragon has been slain (and we'll tell you how to do that later on!) you can come and go as you please, as long as it's through the pre-established portals.

The End is made up of large floating islands of End stone, surrounded by a deadly void. Initially, you arrive on the centre island, which is studded with obsidian pillars and where the dragon lives. This island is surrounded by a huge gap of several hundred empty blocks before a new landscape of islands begins, and this is where you'll find everything else in the End!

TRAVELLING AROUND THE END
Getting around the End is extremely difficult. The islands are spaced quite far apart, so you have to teleport between them if you want to do it with any speed. Gateways teleport you from the centre island to the outer ones, and you can use ender pearls to hop between those.

While it's possible to build bridges

THE END: A NEED TO KNOW GUIDE

The floating islands of the End

The End gateways help you get around

You can make maps in the End

Chorus plants drop fruit

between islands, this is an extremely slow process and very dangerous when you're surrounded by hostile mobs!

SHULKERS
Aside from the dragon and endermen, the only mobs in the End are shulkers. They live inside End cities and resemble purpur blocks, opening to shoot projectiles at you, which inflict the Levitation effect.

NAVIGATING THE END
Just like in the Nether, a compass is no use when travelling in the End unless you have a lodestone. There's no day or night cycle either, so clocks do the same. The one thing you CAN do in the End is make maps, and you should do this as much as possible to make sure you don't lose your bearings. Maps work exactly the same as in the Overworld and will give you a rough idea of where you are in relation to the End gateway that will allow you to teleport home.

Whether you have a map or not, remember not to let yourself get lost. Lay down helpful markers like torches or lamps so you can follow your route home.

BLOCKS
■ **PURPUR** is a decorative block found in End cities and End ships, which you can craft or cut into standard stone shapes like stairs or slabs.
■ **CHORUS PLANTS** are large purple trees that generate in huge amounts. Breaking any part of the tree breaks all blocks attached above it, and potentially drops a chorus fruit.
■ **CHORUS FLOWERS** can be planted in End stone to grow into a chorus plant – not just in the End, but in any dimension.
■ **CHORUS FRUIT** is collected from chorus plants. It's possible to eat chorus fruit to restore four hunger – but it will also teleport you up to eight blocks distance in a random direction! If cooked, chorus fruit become popped chorus fruit, which can be used as part of the crafting recipe for End rods and purpur.
■ **END RODS** are the only light source that exists in the End. They emit light at level 14 and can be placed perpendicular to any surface.

105

The dragon hovering over the exit portal

THE ENDER DRAGON

Before you can leave (or explore!) the End, you have to defeat the fearsome ender dragon

THE DRAGON
The ender dragon is usually the first boss mob you'll face in Minecraft. It may also be the hardest – though the wither is probably scarier! The ender dragon is already nearby when you arrive in the End, and immediately hostile to you. There's no choice but to fight it if you ever want to return to the Overworld.

Before you enter the End, make sure you've got everything you need to defeat the dragon. We recommend strong armour with some good defence enchantments, an Infinity-enchanted bow, and plenty of healing potions and food!

STATS
The dragon has 200 points of health. It has several types of attack, which do differing amounts of damage. The dragon's melee dive does six to 15 damage points. Its wings do three to seven points. Dragon's breath delivers three points of damage for every second you stand in it, and each dragon fireball does six points of damage per hit.

THE ENDER DRAGON

Some ender crystals have iron bars

The ender dragon has 200 health

Destroy the ender crystals

Slaying the dragon

The dragon drops a lot of experience

ENDER CRYSTALS
The first step in killing the dragon is to use a bow and arrow to destroy the ender crystals. These floating blocks are found on top of the tall obsidian pillars dotted around the End. When the dragon gets close to them, they heal its health, so there's no point trying to kill it until they've been taken out.

SLAYING THE DRAGON
After they've all been destroyed, you should hang around near the portal frame. The dragon will swoop down periodically, so dodge its attacks, heal yourself regularly with potions or golden apples, and keep chipping away at its health! It isn't affected by negative status effects like Poison, so save your fancier weapons for fending off any angry endermen nearby.

YOUR REWARDS
Once the dragon is killed, you'll collect a massive 12,000 experience points and gain access to the activated End portal, which will take you back to your spawn point in the Overworld – after showing you the End poem, of course!

You'll also witness the creation of a dragon egg, which sits atop the central spire of a portal frame and teleports away if you try to collect it.

Finally, it will activate an End gateway, allowing you to travel deeper into the End, towards the otherwise inaccessible outer islands and the rewards beyond!

TIPS
Some of the pillars have protective irons bars that you need to climb up and break, but don't hit the ender crystals when you do this – they'll explode in your face!

To collect the egg, you have to make it fall onto something that will cause it to drop as an item. Trick it into teleporting onto End stone, then put two blocks beneath it before breaking the middle block. This will let the egg fall onto the torch and break!

107

END CITIES

An End city exterior

END CITIES

The outer islands of the End are bleak and empty, overrun with chorus trees and endermen – keep exploring to eventually find an End city...

The interiors are confusing!

Watch out for shulkers indoors

FINDING END CITIES

End cities only generate in the outer islands of the End, and even then they're incredibly rare, often with thousands of blocks between them. The best way to find one is to identify the large empty space that separates the central island from the outer island, and explore around the edge of it.

Build a tall structure so you can recognise your starting point, and follow the edge until you arrive at an End city or your original start point. This will provide some bearings from which to mount your search, and there's usually one close to the rim of the outer islands.

END CITY ITEMS

Although similar in nature to villages in the Overworld, End cities are much more complex. They're mostly made of tall towers linked by walkways.

Climbing them is very difficult – sometimes you'll need to parkour your way up, other times you might even need to use the anti-gravity effect of a shulker's attack to float up!

Chests in End cities have the best loot by far. You can expect to see: diamonds, emeralds, saddles, and enchanted tools and armour. You can also collect End rods, which emit light similar to torches but can also be walked on.

END SHIPS

An End ship

A dragon head

The End ship's loot

END SHIPS

The rarest part of an End city, an End ship has the best gear AND a couple of surprises

WHAT ARE END SHIPS?
End ships float near End city walkways. These ships are highly desirable because they contain brewing equipment, chests and – in an item frame below deck – the incredible elytra, which allow you to glide in mid-air!

Not every End city has an End ship attached to it, but you shouldn't have to locate more than two or three to find one that does. Watch out for the masthead too – it's a rare dragon head you won't find anywhere else!

DRAGON HEADS
These decorative heads resemble the actual ender dragon's head, but can be placed as blocks or worn as armour. Wearing a dragon head doesn't prevent you from being seen by the dragon, but it IS pretty scary! If you attach redstone power to a dragon head, it will animate by opening and closing its mouth.

OTHER LOOT
As well as the elytra and dragon head, End ships contain two chests with enchanted armour and tools. You can find iron and diamond items, both with enchantments, as well as ingots and diamonds, saddles, horse armour, emeralds and beetroot seeds. You'll have to fight three shulkers to get at them! There's also a brewing stand with two Instant Health II potions inside. End ships are one of only a couple of places where it's possible to find enchanted diamond gear, so don't leave it behind!

ENDER CHESTS

You can find them in End cities

Items in an ender chest can't be stolen

Ender chests are hard to make, but incredibly useful – learn their secrets here...

Craft several to access items from anywhere

WHAT ARE ENDER CHESTS?
Ender chests contain a single storage area that can be accessed from any other ender chest. This makes them great for transporting rare items large distances without the danger of carrying them yourself. Craft an ender chest at the start and a second when you get where you're going, and you can instantly grab the items placed there originally.

Ender chests contain 27 storage slots, which can be used to store items like any other chest, but every player has access to their own storage area and no one else's. The items in an ender chest can't be shared by players. This means that in multiplayer, one chest can be used by lots of people and will contain different items for each player.

GETTING ENDER CHESTS
To build an ender chest, surround one eye of ender with eight blocks of obsidian on any crafting table. But remember – for the chest to be of use, you have to make at least two!

It's possible to find ender chests in certain End city treasure rooms. However, they can't be mined unless you use a Silk Touch pickaxe – normally they break when mined, dropping eight blocks of obsidian. Remember this when you're transporting your own around – if you don't have another eye of ender, you won't be able to remake it!

SHULKER BOXES

Shulkers hide in purpur blocks

Kill a shulker and collect its shell

Dye them and use them as storage

SHULKER BOXES

Ever feel like you need more storage? Shulker boxes are like having an inventory INSIDE your inventory!

SHULKER BOX USE
Shulker boxes have 27 storage slots, just like a chest, but they keep their items inside when the block is broken. When placed in the inventory, a full shulker box will only take up a single space, and you can access the items inside by placing it in the world, then opening it like you would any other chest.

If you craft lots of shulker boxes, you can increase the amount of items you can carry substantially. They're particularly useful for allowing llamas and horses to transport large numbers of items! Renaming a shulker box on an anvil gets you an achievement, and is useful for labelling their contents.

COLLECTING SHULKER SHELLS
To make a shulker box, you need to collect shulker shells, which are dropped by shulkers. Each shulker has a 50% chance of dropping one when killed so it should be quite easy to collect the two you need! As for chests – if you've made it this far without learning how to craft a chest, you're probably smart enough to figure it out!

CRAFTING A SHULKER BOX
You'll need the following ingredients:
- 2 x Shulker shell
- 1 x Chest (8 x wood planks)

You don't need to do anything special – placed on a crafting table, this will create a shulker box. You can also dye a shulker box one of the standard 16 colours by crafting it with a single piece of dye, and you can remove the dye using a cauldron.

They fold up on your back when not in use

ELYTRA

Ever wished you could fly? Well, if you explore the End, there's a way you can...

FINDING ELYTRA
Elytra are found on End ships, which appear docked in the sky at around half of all End cities, so they're extremely rare! To reach the End ship, you'll need to go up the walkway system, then build your way across to it (or, if you're feeling really daring, wait for a shulker to give you the Anti-gravity effect).

Once you reach the ship, you'll find the elytra stored below deck in the hold. Walk to the back of the ship and you'll spot them in an item frame on the wall. Don't worry – there are no repercussions for grabbing them! This is your reward for making it this far.

ELYTRA USE
Elytra are worn in your inventory armour slot instead of a chestplate. When active, they appear as two large wings on your back, which can unfold when you're in mid-air, allowing you to glide! You can control the

ELYTRA

Elytra are only found on End ships

You can glide long and far

You can use them to glide

Fireworks will propel you upwards

Use phantom membranes to repair elytra

direction and angle of your gliding, and dive to increase the speed. Diving, then pulling back up will give you a little extra height and distance, but you can't stay in the sky forever!

The good news is that if you're using elytra, you won't take fall damage when you land, although it isn't possible to glide indefinitely: for each second of flight the elytra lose one point off their durability value of 431. This means you can glide for seven minutes, 11 seconds using unenchanted ones.

you can let them off while gliding, to propel yourself upwards. This allows something more like actual flight, and lets you cross huge distances at great speeds.

To craft a basic firework rocket, you need one paper and one to three gunpowder. If you're using them for flight, you don't need to add any firework stars, but if you DO it will give a colourful explosion! Carrying a stack of fireworks will mean you can keep propelling yourself around – you can hold 64 in your hand at once.

REPAIRS

When elytra reach a durability value of one, they stop flying. Luckily, unlike most items, they never break completely so you can repair them!

To fix elytra, you can either combine two broken elytra on a grindstone, or patch them with phantom membranes on an anvil. You need four phantom membranes to completely repair a set of elytra.

ENCHANTMENTS

You can also use an anvil to apply the Unbreaking and Mending enchantments, which give them a longer lifespan.

They can also take the Curse of Binding and Curse of Vanishing enchantments – though you'd probably prefer they didn't!

FIREWORKS

Fireworks can be used as decorative items, or as more powerful ammo in a crossbow – but they REALLY become useful when you're using them while flying around with elytra. Place them in your main hand, and

114

ADVANCED MINECRAFT

115

Everything you need to start brewing

BREWING

You may have found potions in the game – but how about making your own?

BREWING EQUIPMENT
Potions allow you to power yourself up with temporary stats boosts and permanent health effects. They can also be used to weaken and harm enemies. While you can find a few in the game, you'll mostly have to make them yourself by brewing.

To start brewing, you need to either craft a brewing stand (using a blaze rod and three cobblestone blocks), or collect one from a village church or igloo basement.

You'll also need several glass bottles (craft three bottles from three glass blocks), a water source and some blaze powder. You also need your potion ingredients!

BASE POTIONS
To make a base potion, fill your glass bottles with water and place them into a brewing stand, then put blaze powder into the fuel slot. Now, add Nether wart to create an awkward potion.

If you don't add Nether wart, you can only craft mundane and thick potions, which are useless, or a Potion of Weakness (by adding a fermented spider eye, made from sugar, a mushroom and a spider eye).

However, you can add all of the following to an awkward potion to create something with a more powerful effect:
- Sugar = Swiftness
- Rabbit's foot = Leaping
- Glistering melon = Healing

BREWING

Find a brewing stand in an igloo basement

Splash and lingering potions affect several mobs together

Always add Nether wart first

Collect dragon's breath for lingering potions

Gunpowder makes splash potions

- Spider eye = Poison
- Pufferfish = Water Breathing
- Magma cream = Fire Resistance
- Golden carrot = Night Vision
- Blaze powder = Strength
- Ghast tear = Regeneration
- Turtle shell = Turtle Master
- Phantom membrane = Slow Falling

Most potions brewed at this stage have effects that last for about three minutes, but some last for as little as 45 seconds.

EXTENDED POTIONS

To create better potions, add redstone (which roughly doubles the time a potion works) or glowstone dust (which makes the effect stronger but halves the time it lasts).

Adding gunpowder turns the potion into a splash potion, which can be thrown as a weapon or to affect multiple friendly players at once. The effect of a splash potion extends four blocks in every direction from the place the potion smashed, and a direct hit will give 100% of the potion's effect. This decreases the further a player or mob is from the potion when it breaks.

Adding dragon's breath creates a lingering potion, which can also be thrown and will persist on the ground. Dragon's breath can only be collected from the ground while fighting the ender dragon, so it's very hard to get! Lingering potions only give effects that last for about half as long as a drinkable potion, but it's easier for lots of mobs/players to be affected.

You can also use fermented spider eyes to "corrupt" a potion's effects:
- A Potion of Night Vision becomes a Potion of Invisibility
- A Potion of Swiftness or Leaping become a Potion of Slowness
- A Potion of Healing or Poison become a Potion of Harming

Most potions are good or bad, but the Potion of the Turtle Master gives you both the Slowness AND Resistance effects, so you're 40% slower but also 60% harder to injure. When the potion is enhanced with glowstone, you get just 10% of your normal speed, but the resistance effect is 80%.

117

Enchanted gear has special powers

Enchanting GEAR

Enchanting gear can make it faster, stronger, or just generally more fun to use – here's how you do it

ENCHANTING TABLES
Enchantments make your weapons and armour more effective and give you special abilities that you can use while wearing it. Learning to use enchantments is important if you want to reach (and survive!) the game's harder areas!

The easiest way to enchant items is with an enchanting table. To enchant items, you need the following:

- An enchanting table (four obsidian, two diamond, one book)
- One to three Lapis lazuli pieces per enchantment
- Several experience levels
- An item that accepts enchantments (tools, armour and books)
- Optionally, some bookshelves (six wood planks, three books each)

When placed around an enchantment table, bookshelves increase the level an enchantment can reach. You do have to spend more lapis lazuli and experience points to get higher level enchantments,

ENCHANTING GEAR

Look out for the purple glow!

A fully powered enchanting table

You can't choose the exact enchantment

Anvils let you put the best enchantments onto items

The Mending enchantment is only available on a book

though! When powering up enchantments using bookshelves, there's an upper limit of 15. Any additional bookshelves you place will have no effect on the strength of the enchantments.

When you're ready, place your tool, armour or book onto the table along with up to three pieces of lapis lazuli. You can then "spend" your experience points along with the lapis lazuli to cast an enchantment.

Unfortunately, there's no way of knowing what an enchantment is before you apply it – it's determined by some very complex algorithms! Generally, you get higher level enchantments if the item is made of gold and if you have lots of bookshelves powering the table up. More powerful enchantments may apply several different types at once.

ENCHANTING BOOKS

It's possible to choose the enchantment you want to apply to an item by using an enchanted book on an anvil. Books can hold enchantments for safekeeping, and you can enchant them directly to see what you've got – it makes sure you don't apply a weak or uninteresting enchantment to a valuable tool or weapon.

The process isn't that different to enchanting any other item: first use the enchanting table as you would normally, but instead of placing the spell on your item, place it on a book.

When you have the item you want to enchant and a book with the enchantment you want, combine the two on an anvil for a small experience cost. The same process also allows you to add enchantments to items that can't be placed on an enchanting table, such as shears.

ENCHANTING TIPS & TRICKS

Books are the only item that can take any enchantment. If you combine two enchanted items on an anvil, the resulting item will have both enchantments.

As well as the additional experience cost of using the anvil, you lose out slightly when enchanting books because they won't receive enchantments with as high a level as if the tool or item was being enchanted itself.

You can combine two books with the same type (and level) of enchantment to level it up (e.g. combining two books with Sharpness II would create one book with Sharpness III).

119

The wither has a lot of health

Summoning
THE WITHER

The wither is the most terrifying boss mob in all of Minecraft, and that's made worse by the knowledge that only you can choose to summon it. You did this to yourself!

SUMMONING A WITHER

You can summon the wither at any time by placing four blocks of soul sand or soul soil in a "T" shape, with three wither skeleton skulls on the top row. Soul sand and soul soil are easy to find in the Nether, but the skulls can only be found by killing large numbers of wither skeletons. It takes around 120 wither skeleton kills to get three wither skeleton skulls.

If you've built the totem correctly (and you're not in Peaceful mode), it will turn into a white wither as it crosses over into our dimension from wherever it exists. When the wither properly awakens, it will cause a large explosion that damages anything close by, so get out of the way once the third head is placed!

Prepare for a difficult fight – when active, the wither is hostile to all mobs except

120

SUMMONING THE WITHER

This painting shows how to summon the wither

You never want to get this close!

Build this from soul sand and wither skulls

Then get ready to run!

When it loses half its health, it gets armour

zombies and skeletons. It might be worth building a lot of golems to try to draw its fire. Maxed out health, armour and weaponry are also a must! Don't summon a wither too close to anything important – it will destroy most blocks that it touches. Only End portal frames and bedrock are immune!

Whatever you choose to fight the wither with, you'll also need a lot of good luck to beat it...

WITHER STATS

The wither has 300 health points in the PC and Console Editions, and 600 in the Pocket Edition. It's 3.5 blocks high, and has an attack strength that varies with the difficulty. On Easy mode, its attacks do five damage, on Normal they do eight damage, and on Hard they do 12 damage.

Its Wither Skull attack causes explosions and poisons mobs, and on Normal and Hard difficulties it inflicts the Wither effect too, which drains health while turning your health hearts black so you can't see how many you have. The wither's attacks also leave a wither rose on the ground, which can cause the Wither effect if you stand too close to it.

Killing the wither causes it to drop a Nether star, which you can use to create beacons. You can summon and kill the wither as many times as you like – but once is usually enough! You also get 50 experience for successfully killing the wither.

WITHER TIPS & SECRETS

One of the game's random paintings shows the structure needed to summon a wither, which is a clue to players as to how they summon it. Images of the wither also appear on red chiselled sandstone.

The wither is technically undead, meaning it can be hurt by splash Potions of Healing.

The Wither can't be hurt by lava or drowning, nor attacks from any undead mob.

Kill a banner-holding captain to get cursed…

Pillager RAIDS

Pillagers are tough enough to fight in their outposts or when you encounter them as patrols – but now they're also coming to attack your village…

HOW A RAID STARTS
When you encounter pillagers, one in the party will carry an illager banner. This is the leader of that group. If you kill the leader, they drop their normal items as well as their banner, but something else happens: you're given the Bad Omen status effect.

The Bad Omen effect makes it more likely that a village will be raided the next time you enter it. Each leader you kill adds a level to your Bad Omen status effect to a maximum of level six, so killing multiple leaders will make the raids worse and worse. A level six raid means you and the villagers will have to survive ten waves of attacks. That's tough even if you're fully tooled up!

WHAT HAPPENS IN A RAID
If a raid starts, you'll see waves of enemies – mostly pillagers and vindicators – attacking the village you've just entered, going door to door to try to kill the villagers. Pillagers prefer to attack villagers when they can, but they'll change targets if attacked by another entity,

122

PILLAGER RAIDS

...then it's bad news next time you enter a village

You'll fight a lot of mobs!

Watch out for ravagers

Even witches join in!

Kill them all and you'll be a hero

whether that's a player, golem or another mob, so the best way to save the village is to draw the pillagers' attention to yourself.

In some waves, the attacking illagers will be joined by ravagers – and these large, bull-like creatures are seriously bad news.

RAVAGERS
Ravagers resemble large armoured bulls, and can only be ridden by pillagers. They're hostile to any players, iron golems, villagers and traders that get within 16 blocks and will ram them, dealing 12 points of damage and a huge amount of knockback.

If a ravager is stunned (for example, if its attack is blocked by a shield), it will be still for two seconds, then emit a roar that does six points of damage to all nearby entities. This can cause illagers to turn on the beasts!

Ravagers destroy any leaves or crops they come into contact with, trampling them quickly. They have 100 health points, so if you spot them it's best to start attacking fast!

HERO OF THE VILLAGE
Every redesigned village now features a village bell, which if rung during a raid will apply the Glowing effect to any illagers within a 32-block radius and cause nearby villagers to run for their houses to (relative) safety. The glowing effect makes it easier to find and kill the attackers.

If you succeed in ending the raid, you'll receive the Hero of the Village status effect, which will last for 60 minutes (or until you leave the village) and causes traders to give you a discount of between 30% and 55%, depending on the level of the status effect. Items can't be discounted below a cost of one emerald, and the level of the status effect is determined by the level of Bad Omen the player had when the raid was originally caused.

123

Most villagers will hide indoors

Zombie SIEGES

Think you're safe in a village because you haven't killed any pillager leaders? Bad news: you can still be attacked by zombies in a siege

WHAT CAUSES A SIEGE?

Unless you spend a lot of time hanging around in villages overnight, you probably won't have experienced a zombie siege event because they're quite rare. On the surface, they seem to happen almost at random, but there are some things that can trigger them. Sieges will only start in villages that have ten beds and 20 villagers, so you also need to make sure the villages you're waiting in are quite large!

A siege can occur in any village, no matter how well lit or well defended it is. Each night, at exactly midnight (18000 on the Minecraft clock), the game has a one in ten chance of trying to start a siege. From

ZOMBIE SIEGES

Sieges can start on any night

Nowhere is safe!

A siege can overrun a whole village

The local golem will help out

Sieges only happen in large villages

that point on, it attempts to start one every second until dawn begins – or, specifically, when the light level reaches 12, so rain can allow sieges to start well into the day!

That means if you want a siege event to begin, you need to make sure you're in a village every night at midnight game time. You should only have to do it for a maximum of ten nights to get at least one siege, but it isn't guaranteed – if you did it for 100 nights, you'd probably have ten sieges, but they might all happen after 50 nights without one!

WHAT HAPPENS IN A SIEGE?

When the event activates, zombies will spawn in huge numbers within the village itself and begin attacking. During a siege, up to 20 zombies will spawn within three seconds. These zombies are unaffected by light or the presence of other mobs, and will even behave more aggressively than other zombies! Husks and zombie villagers never spawn as part of a siege, but other variants (such as baby zombies and chicken jockeys) can.

A siege ends when all the zombies are killed, whether by the player or because they burn up in the sunlight. Unlike raids, there are no special effects gained from defeating a siege! If a siege starts when you're in a village, you should intervene – it's virtually guaranteed that the village will be wiped out if you don't!

SIEGE RECOVERY

If villagers die during a siege but at least two villagers remain alive, they'll mate and gradually repopulate the village. No new sieges will occur until the population reaches at least 20. If fewer than two villagers survive, it's possible (though difficult!) to repopulate a village by luring zombie villagers there and then curing them, or by transporting villagers from other nearby villages. Of course, you could always cheat and use the village spawn egg in Creative mode!

If you want to avoid a siege happening while you're in a village, the best tactic is to sleep in a bed as soon as it gets dark!

A full conduit frame

CONDUITS

Want to establish an underwater base? You need to think about a conduit, which is kind of like an underwater beacon!

CRAFTING A CONDUIT
The first thing you need to do is collect raw materials. To build a complete conduit, you need:
- One Heart of the sea
- Eight Nautilus shells
- Up to 42 prismarine-type blocks

Collecting a heart of the sea is fairly simple – they're commonly found in buried treasure chests!

Nautilus shells are the hardest part of the conduit to get hold of. You can collect one by killing a drowned that is carrying one, as a treasure item when fishing, from treasure chests, or by trading with a wandering trader.

The prismarine blocks can be any type of full-block prismarine variant – regular, dark, bricks or even sea lanterns – but not slabs, stairs or double slabs. Get them from any ocean monument.

ACTIVATION
Making a conduit is simple: using a crafting table, surround the heart of the sea with nautilus shells to craft a conduit block. Place it underwater and build a conduit frame around it to activate it. You can place a conduit on land, but it won't have any effect!

When a conduit is placed, it will emit a light of level 15. If activated (i.e. placed underwater inside a frame), it will also give out the Conduit Power effect for a range of 32 blocks in every direction.

CONDUITS

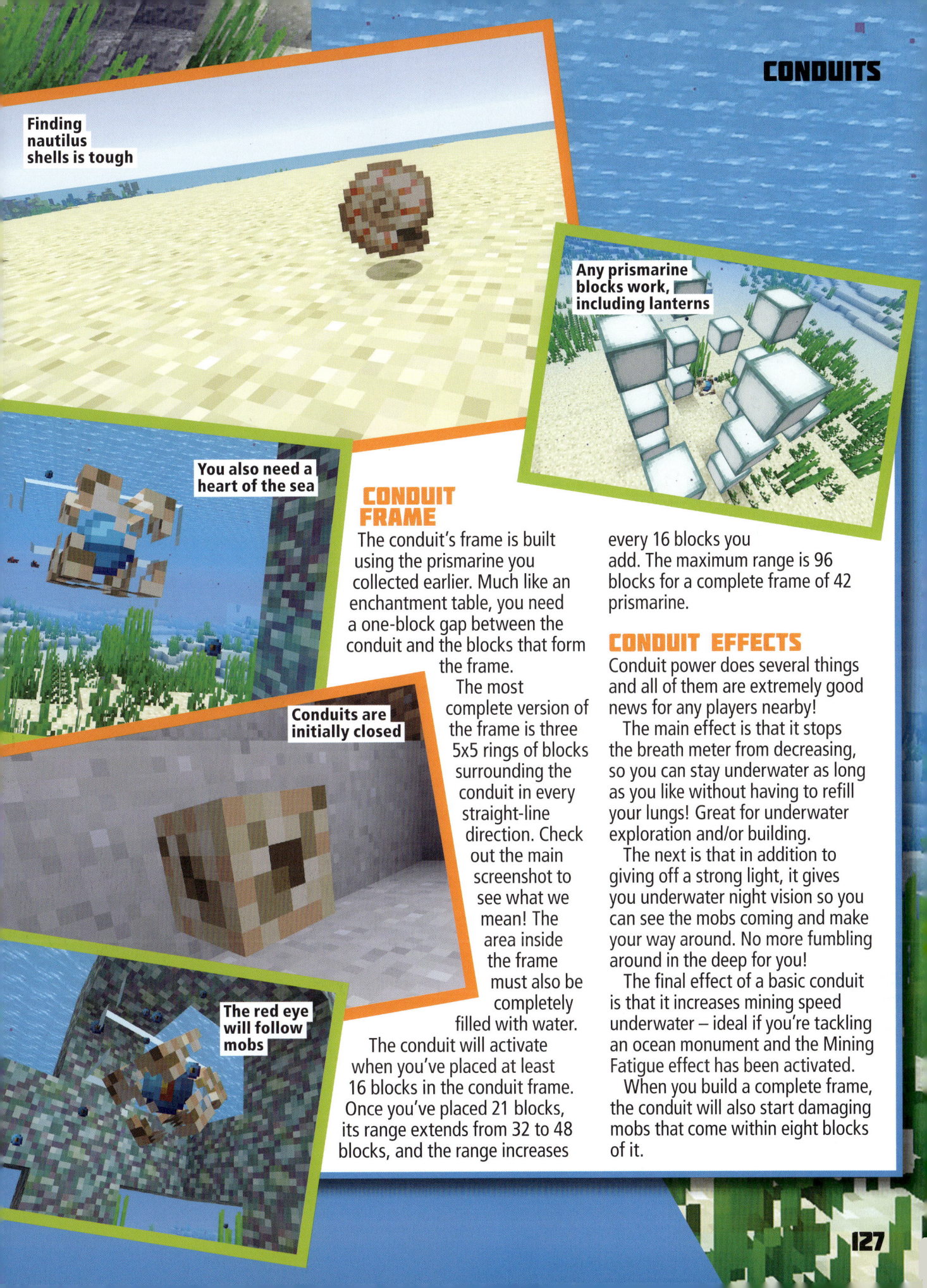

Finding nautilus shells is tough

Any prismarine blocks work, including lanterns

You also need a heart of the sea

Conduits are initially closed

The red eye will follow mobs

CONDUIT FRAME

The conduit's frame is built using the prismarine you collected earlier. Much like an enchantment table, you need a one-block gap between the conduit and the blocks that form the frame.

The most complete version of the frame is three 5x5 rings of blocks surrounding the conduit in every straight-line direction. Check out the main screenshot to see what we mean! The area inside the frame must also be completely filled with water.

The conduit will activate when you've placed at least 16 blocks in the conduit frame. Once you've placed 21 blocks, its range extends from 32 to 48 blocks, and the range increases every 16 blocks you add. The maximum range is 96 blocks for a complete frame of 42 prismarine.

CONDUIT EFFECTS

Conduit power does several things and all of them are extremely good news for any players nearby!

The main effect is that it stops the breath meter from decreasing, so you can stay underwater as long as you like without having to refill your lungs! Great for underwater exploration and/or building.

The next is that in addition to giving off a strong light, it gives you underwater night vision so you can see the mobs coming and make your way around. No more fumbling around in the deep for you!

The final effect of a basic conduit is that it increases mining speed underwater – ideal if you're tackling an ocean monument and the Mining Fatigue effect has been activated.

When you build a complete frame, the conduit will also start damaging mobs that come within eight blocks of it.

You can mix and match beacon materials

Light a BEACON

What's that in the sky? Is it a bird? A plane? No, it's a strange beam of light!

The powers of a full beacon

BEACON MATERIALS
The ultimate monument to your complete mastery of Minecraft, beacons look amazing, are useful as a navigation tool, and give you positive status effects when you're close by.

To create a beacon, you'll need at least nine iron, gold, emerald, diamond or Netherite blocks, each of which is crafted from nine ingots of gems. The material makes no difference to how the beacon behaves – you can mix and match these blocks however you like (e.g. you could have three iron blocks, two gold blocks and four emerald blocks), but nine is the smallest amount you can make a beacon with.

You also need to craft a beacon block, which you can do with three obsidian, one Nether star and five glass blocks. Note that to collect a Nether star, you must awaken and defeat the wither, so it's fair to say it's not easy!

LIGHT A BEACON

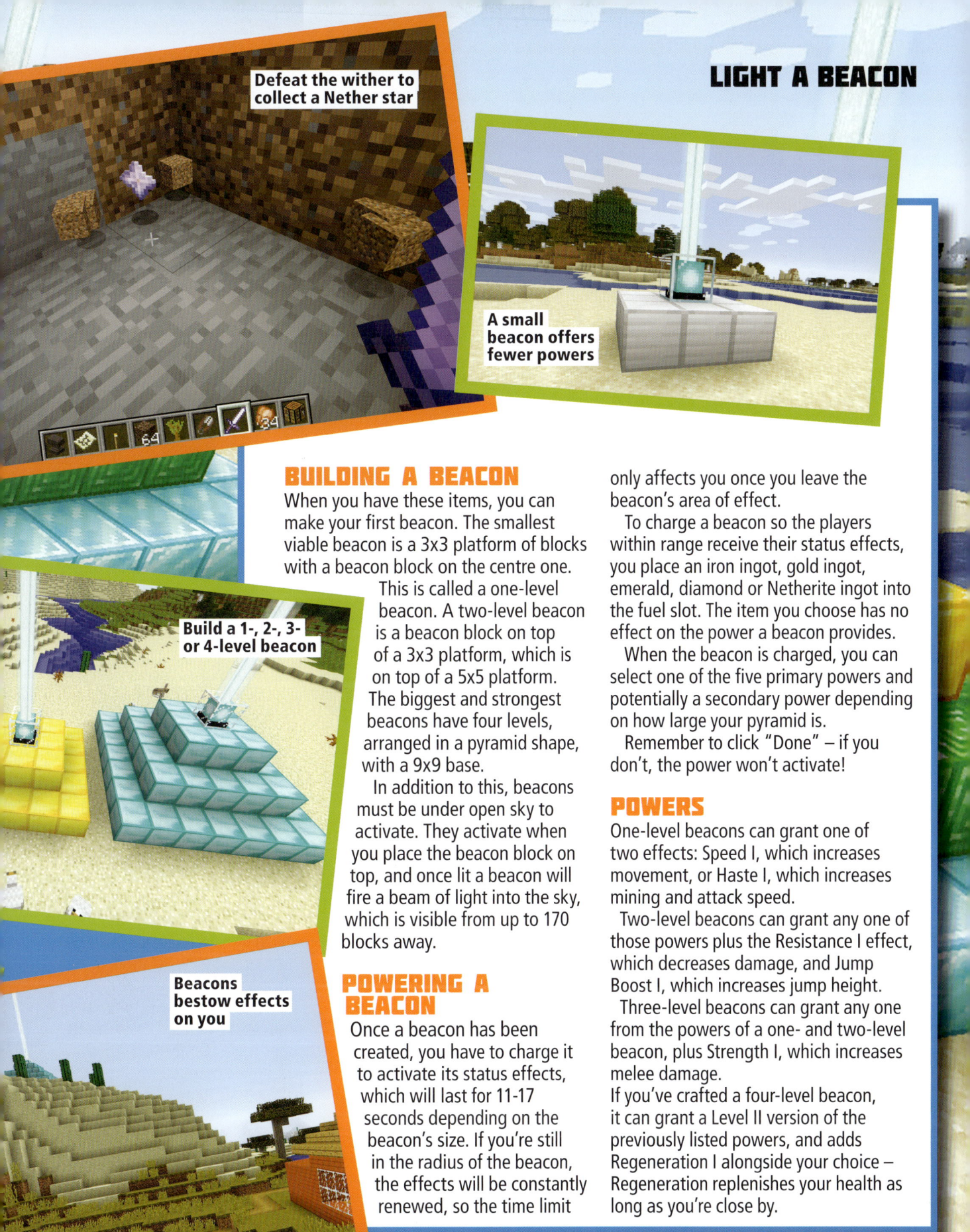

Defeat the wither to collect a Nether star

A small beacon offers fewer powers

Build a 1-, 2-, 3- or 4-level beacon

Beacons bestow effects on you

BUILDING A BEACON
When you have these items, you can make your first beacon. The smallest viable beacon is a 3x3 platform of blocks with a beacon block on the centre one.

This is called a one-level beacon. A two-level beacon is a beacon block on top of a 3x3 platform, which is on top of a 5x5 platform. The biggest and strongest beacons have four levels, arranged in a pyramid shape, with a 9x9 base.

In addition to this, beacons must be under open sky to activate. They activate when you place the beacon block on top, and once lit a beacon will fire a beam of light into the sky, which is visible from up to 170 blocks away.

POWERING A BEACON
Once a beacon has been created, you have to charge it to activate its status effects, which will last for 11-17 seconds depending on the beacon's size. If you're still in the radius of the beacon, the effects will be constantly renewed, so the time limit only affects you once you leave the beacon's area of effect.

To charge a beacon so the players within range receive their status effects, you place an iron ingot, gold ingot, emerald, diamond or Netherite ingot into the fuel slot. The item you choose has no effect on the power a beacon provides.

When the beacon is charged, you can select one of the five primary powers and potentially a secondary power depending on how large your pyramid is.

Remember to click "Done" – if you don't, the power won't activate!

POWERS
One-level beacons can grant one of two effects: Speed I, which increases movement, or Haste I, which increases mining and attack speed.

Two-level beacons can grant any one of those powers plus the Resistance I effect, which decreases damage, and Jump Boost I, which increases jump height.

Three-level beacons can grant any one from the powers of a one- and two-level beacon, plus Strength I, which increases melee damage.

If you've crafted a four-level beacon, it can grant a Level II version of the previously listed powers, and adds Regeneration I alongside your choice – Regeneration replenishes your health as long as you're close by.

If you want to fight the dragon again, do this...

RESPAWN THE DRAGON

Does the End seem a little too safe to you now? Well, we've got good news...

BRING BACK THE DRAGON
The ender dragon is one of the toughest foes, and there's only ever one in your world at any time. Once you've killed it, you might think all the fun's over. Well, that's not the case. If you want to fight the dragon again, you can respawn it.

HOW TO DO IT
Summoning a new dragon is fairly easy: you have to craft four End crystals, then place one on each side of the exit portal that allows you to leave the End – the one that the egg appears on top of.

(Note that you do NOT need a dragon egg in your possession, or even close by, in order to respawn the dragon. The egg is purely a trophy and/or cosmetic item.)

To craft an End crystal, you need to place an eye of ender in the centre of a crafting table, a ghast tear below it, and glass blocks in the remaining slots.

RESPAWN THE DRAGON

The crystals will summon a new one

Maybe you just want a fight

The only place you can find End crystals

Respawn the dragon to collect dragon's breath

Again, it takes four of these crystals to revive the dragon, so expect to spend a lot of time in the Nether looking for items!

If you place the crystals, several things will happen. The dragon will respawn, for a start, but the obsidian pillars and End crystals will regenerate too. More upsettingly, the exit portal will deactivate – so once you've respawned the dragon, you can't leave the End until it's beaten again!

WHY RESPAWN THE DRAGON?

The primary reason to respawn the ender dragon is if you want to get your hands on some dragon's breath. Once the dragon's been killed, there's no way to obtain dragon's breath in Survival mode. Respawning the dragon is fun, but it's also the one chance you have of creating lingering potions!

Another good reason to respawn the dragon is that each time you kill it, a new End gateway generates. This gives you a chance to explore the outer islands of the End from a new vantage point. You can have up to 20 End gateways spawned before the number caps out.

Of course, you also get additional experience for killing the dragon, so don't overlook that. And, hey, maybe you just like a challenge! Whatever your reason, you'll find that each time you beat the dragon, you get a little better at doing it.

CHANGES

Slaying the dragon a second time isn't quite the same as the first time. For a start, you miss out on the egg. You're only given a dragon egg to collect the first time you slay the dragon – there will only ever be one true egg in a Survival mode game.

The second major thing to note is that you only get 500 experience for each subsequent time you kill the dragon, which can seem stingy after the 12,000 points drop of the first dragon death – but it's still higher than anything else in the game!

The portal will deactivate until you kill the dragon

A vindicator called Johnny

ADVANCED CHEATS & SECRETS

Think you know all there is to know about Minecraft? Well, if you've read this far, you probably know a lot – but there are still some things we have left to teach you…!

>> If you use a name tag to call a Vindicator "Johnny", it will be hostile to any other mob, except for other illagers. This is a reference to the old horror movie, *The Shining*.

>> If you use a name tag on a sheep to rename it "jeb_" (no capitals, with the underscore), its wool will cycle through every available colour.

>> On 31st October, any mob that can wear armour – zombies, skeletons, pigmen and wither skeletons – can spawn wearing a pumpkin or Jack O'Lantern.

>> A variant mob can be created by using a name tag to call a rabbit "Toast" (with the capital letter).

>> A maximum-power conduit has a range of 96 blocks and will give players underwater night vision, faster underwater mining and infinite underwater breath.

ADVANCED CHEATS & SECRETS

Conduits have a 96-block range

Dragon heads move if connected to redstone

You always find a heart in buried treasure

A pig called Dinnerbone

The moon and sun both travel in the same direction

» There's a tiny chance (one in 10,000 launches) that the title screen will read "Minceraft" instead of Minecraft. It was added to the game by the original developer, Notch, but nobody noticed for years!

» If you connect a dragon head to a redstone power source, you can make it open and close its mouth.

» Placing a block of coloured glass in the beam of a beacon will make it change to the same colour of the glass block.

» In the Java Edition, a conduit's effects are carried through rain as well as solid water, but this doesn't (at the time of writing) apply in the Bedrock Edition.

» Conduits have an eye that will show whether they're hunting for hostile mobs or not. If it's open, it's hunting for hostile mobs. If not, it will be closed.

» Activating a conduit will give you the Moskstraumen achievement. The Moskstraumen is a series of whirlpools that exist in the real world off the coast of Norway.

» Complete conduits cause four points of damage every two seconds – but only as long as they and the mobs are both in contact with water.

» The nautilus shell and heart of the sea have no other use in the game aside from crafting conduits!

» All buried treasure chests contain a heart of the sea, so you shouldn't have to look far to find one! You'll get the Me Gold! achievement for finding a buried treasure chest.

» Although you can activate a conduit by building a complete ring around it, you can place any 16 blocks in valid frame locations and it will work.

» If you use a name tag to give a mob the name "Dinnerbone" or "Grumm" (with capital letters), it turns upside down. Dinnerbone and Grumm are two of Minecraft's developers!

» At night, the moon and stars travel in the same direction as Minecraft's sun: from east to west. If you don't have a compass or map, you can use the moon to navigate roughly in the direction you need to go.

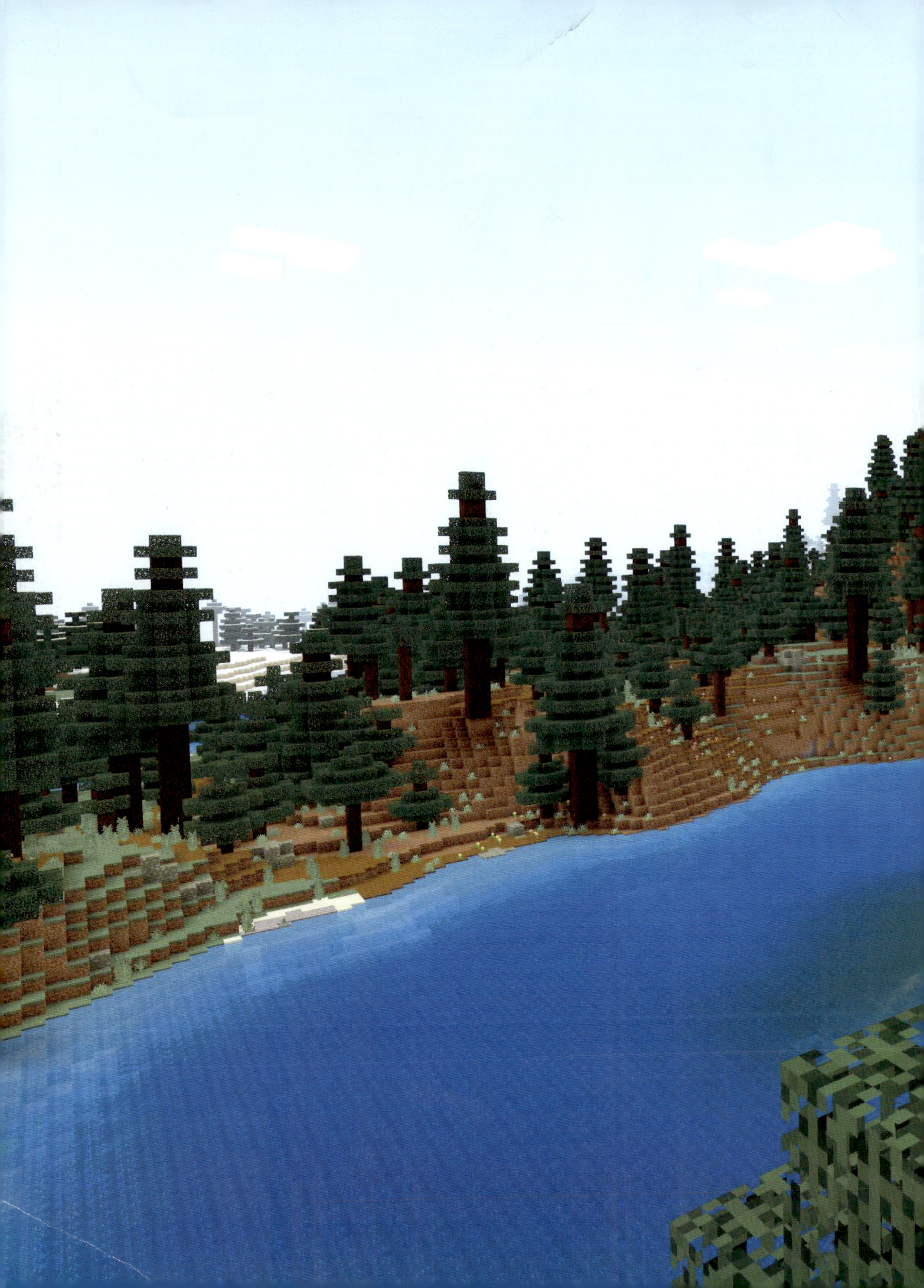